# Our
# Otherness
# Is Our
# Strength

# Our *Otherness* Is Our *Strength*

Wisdom from the
Boogie Down Bronx

Andrea Navedo

BROADLEAF BOOKS
MINNEAPOLIS

Library of Congress Cataloging-in-Publication Data

Names: Navedo, Andrea, author.
Title: Our otherness is our strength : wisdom from the boogie down
    Bronx / Andrea Navedo.
Identifiers: LCCN 2022054662 (print) | LCCN 2022054663 (ebook) |
    ISBN 9781506485706 (hardcover) | ISBN 9781506485713 (ebook)
Subjects: LCSH: Self-actualization (Psychology) | Other (Philosophy) |
    Identity (Psychology) | Navedo, Andrea, 1969- | Hispanic American
    women--Social conditions.
Classification: LCC BF637.S4 N376 2023 (print) | LCC BF637.S4 (ebook) |
    DDC 158.1--dc23/eng/20221116
LC record available at https://lccn.loc.gov/2022054662
LC ebook record available at https://lccn.loc.gov/2022054663

Andrea Navedo photo by Diana Ragland
Cover image: © Getty Images 2022; New York City Skyline Silhouette Vector
Illustration by vladmarko
Cover design: 1517 Media

Print ISBN: 978-1-5064-8570-6
eBook ISBN: 978-1-5064-8571-3
Printed in China

*For Ava and Nico:*

*I hope these stories inspire you to fight for you,
to love yourself, and to be the captains of your ship.*

# Contents

## CONTENTS

## *Note to the Reader*

I was one of the girls recruited to attend the once-famous Dewitt Clinton High School in The Bronx to make it co-ed to "save" it from being shut down. It had a long history as an all-boys school, stretching all the way back to 1897, with many notable alumni including Judd Hirsch, from the hit TV show *Taxi,* and Ralph Lauren, the clothing designer. In 1983 the school was deemed a school that was failing and threatened with being shut down. To try to salvage the school, a proposal was made to make it co-ed. I thought they had made a mistake by enrolling me in that first co-ed class. Little did I know that thirty years later I would be invited as a celebrity guest to give a commencement speech. My life had come full circle. I was so happy to come back to share some of my trials and hopefully help give a leg up to those students sitting in the same seats, facing the same issues, that I had way back when.

"If we are honest with ourselves, we must admit that the only thing we truly own is our lives, and it is what we do with our lives that determines what kind of people we are."
~Cesar Chavez

"Don't worry, I believe in you almost as much as I believe in myself."

~Rogelio De La Vega
*Jane the Virgin*

# Your "Otherness" Is Your Strength

When you hear someone say, "I want to become an actor," you might roll your eyes and think, "Yeah, good luck with that!" Born and bred in The Bronx, I believed becoming an actor was an impossible goal for me until I realized that growing up in da South Bronx—the boogie down, the burning borough of New York City—brought out my superpowers.

I knew the odds were stacked against me. I'm Latina, "brown," the "other." I didn't get to see many positive portrayals of Latinas in the media growing up. I was keenly aware that I was not what mainstream media valued. Add to that the disheartening fact that only 5 percent of actors earn enough to make a living. I could have let all that get in my way. But I decided that was not how it was going to go down. Not with me. My difference, or what I like to call my "otherness," was my strength. My circumstances and heritage were different from what I saw on TV and film, but goddammit, I was going to hold onto them and claim them with pride. They had given me so much. Growing up brown in The Bronx taught me how to survive, how to fight, both literally and figuratively. It conditioned me to strive and go the distance, to persevere, to be tenacious. It groomed me to read people, situations, and circumstances and gave me a strong intuition that keeps me safe. It trained me to keep my feet on the ground, stay humble, keep it real, and be grateful. Growing up in the South Bronx equipped me with the qualities I needed to chase that next-to-impossible career of acting.

I just didn't think that chase would take twenty-seven years! As a working actor, it was twenty-seven years of pounding the pavement, getting headshots, audition after audition, endless rejection, doing plays, acting classes, rehearsals, and practice over and over, simultaneous with trying to have a life: getting married, having children, and trying to pay the rent on time. All of that finally led to booking my first series-regular role in *Jane the Virgin*.

Had I believed the statistics and that I was a victim of what films, books, and media have wrongly identified as the horrors of The Bronx, had I listened to the negativity from the outside world and within my own mind, I would not have had the immense pleasure of being part of such a groundbreaking show. I would never have had the opportunity to play a role that portrayed a Latina single mother as complex, flawed, and genuine. Nor would I have had the immense pleasure of representing my beautiful Latina heritage on mainstream TV. The long, difficult journey was so worth it. And looking back now, I know that embracing my "otherness" is what got me where I am today. The "ghetto" was my training ground for self-actualization. Hardship, trauma, discrimination, and inner fears and doubts from that "ghetto" upbringing developed in me secret weapons that equipped me to triumph.

Latina, brown, South-Bronx born and bred, my otherness makes me unique and gives me something different to contribute to the world. My otherness makes me appreciate the difference of those who aren't like me; how boring life would be if we were all alike.

Never in my wildest dreams did I think telling my Bronx stories and what they taught me would be part of my journey. But I am happy to share them with you. I know the otherness pains of regret, holding myself back, being stuck. The otherness pain of not feeling that I matter. The otherness pain of not loving myself. I had to learn to listen compassionately to my own internal dialogue and teach my whole self these new statements to replace what I used to say to myself:

- I embrace where I'm from and I will risk finding where I really belong.

3

- I have to want my dreams more than anyone else.
- I have to choose myself before anyone else will choose me.
- Words have power. I use them in my own voice and declare with emotion what I want.
- My "otherness" is not an obstacle to be overcome. My "otherness" *is* my strength.

"Fear of failure, that's what it was. Which can be a very crippling thing."

~Rogelio De La Vega
*Jane the Virgin*

# Fear Is a Mofo, Step Up to the Plate Anyway

People ask me how I got the part of Xiomara on *Jane the Virgin* and they usually expect the normal story about auditioning. But my story entails much more than that. It begins with a war in my mind, a battle against fear, and a struggle to gather the courage to win.

In November of 2013, I was in Los Angeles and had been working with a new manager, Norman Aladjem, for about six months. I'd just finished filming the action-comedy parody of the *The Fast and the Furious* series called *Superfast!* I played the role of Michelle Rodriguez. Norman arranged general meetings for me with the different networks in order to lay the groundwork for the upcoming pilot season. Then it was time for me to go back home to my kids and husband in New York. However, before I left, my managers repeatedly encouraged me to return to LA for pilot season. They felt that me being in the room in person with the casting directors was key. Pilot season, which usually starts in February and lasts about six weeks, is when TV networks cast for new upcoming shows.

Shortly after I returned to New York, my mother-in-law ended up in the hospital. A week later, my father-in-law went into the hospital. They were both in their mid-eighties. While my father-in-law was in the hospital, they found out he had liver cancer. He passed away ten days after that. My children were little and my husband was running a business. It was a very tough time. Extremely stressful. I knew my managers would be calling me soon to say, "It's time. Pilot season is coming up. You really need to come out to LA. It's going make all the difference."

I knew in my heart that they were right. Nonetheless it was a real internal struggle for me. "What are people going to think if you leave your husband and two kids while his mom is in the hospital and the whole family is mourning his father's passing, just so that you can go off and audition? What kind of mother are you to leave your kids for a month? What kind of wife are you?"

Even though I was afraid to talk to my husband about it, I finally did. It was a risk I was willing to take. I knew I had to shake things up, do a different dance step, pick myself, take a bet on me, get out of my comfort zone. "How do you feel about me going away for pilot season?" I asked him. "My managers really think it's going make all the difference."

"Go. I got this," he said. "I got home base covered."

And you know what? I didn't believe him. I thought he was testing me. I thought he was testing my love for him. I went a whole two weeks more torturing myself about whether or not to go to LA for pilot season, telling myself that I had to talk with my husband, as if we hadn't already had the conversation! Two weeks later I approached him again. "Babe, I've got to go to LA. I have to go. My managers say it's going to make all the difference."

"I told you to go. I got this covered."

"Really?"

"Yes, Andrea. Just go."

So I said to myself, "Okay. I have to take action before I back out of this again." I ran to my computer and ordered my plane tickets to LA. Boom! That was done. Then I called my manager: "Norman, I'm coming out. Here are the dates, I need a car." He replied, "I got a car for you." Boom! That fell into place. I needed babysitting. I made more calls. Boom! That fell into place too. The stars aligned; it all fell into place once I put aside my fear of what people would think and dared to take a risk.

One week later, I boarded the plane to LA. I sat in my seat looking out the window. As the plane started to take off, a peace came over me. My anxieties dissipated. I felt calm, even happy. I knew in my heart that I was where I was supposed to be. I knew I wasn't a bad mother. I knew I wasn't a bad wife. And I realized those were just excuses. The truth was I was afraid to fail. I was afraid that after leaving my family in that situation, going away for a month, spending all that money, I would come back with nothing. I would be embarrassed. I would feel like a loser. As the plane gained altitude, I allowed that truth to sink in. Then I said to myself, "I'm good with whatever happens on this trip because you know what? I already won. I won the battle against fear. In spite of all my doubts and fears, I took the risk. Fear didn't stop me from taking action. I am on my way. I am sitting on this plane on my way to LA. What will happen? I don't know, but I'm ready to accept whatever the outcome is. I won't look back with regret because I already won. I won the battle against fear. I am at peace."

Three days after I landed in LA, I got my first audition. It was for *Jane the Virgin*—the role of Xiomara. As I prepared the scenes, I immediately identified with her. I understood her. A single mom trying to be the best mom she can be, all the while still pursuing her big dream of becoming a professional singer. I drilled the mother-effing-shit out of those scenes, let me tell you. I prepared like there was no tomorrow. I went into that audition a little scared, but I understood Xiomara. I was in the zone and I knew it. I kicked ass! The producers smiled and laughed as I landed the jokes. They seemed excited. I left the room feeling like I had just gotten off a rollercoaster ride.

Thirty minutes later I got a call from Norman. "How did it go?"

"Not sure, but I think it went well."

"How long ago did you leave?"

"About thirty minutes ago."

"Well, they called about fifteen minutes ago asking you to screen test."

"What? Really? Oh my god!"

My first audition in LA had become a screen test and one month later, after several screen tests and a chemistry read with Gina Rodriguez, I booked the role of Xiomara on *Jane the Virgin*—exactly within the time period of my round-trip ticket from New York.

Once I made the decision to go to LA despite my fears, all the pieces fell into place, as if part of some divine plan. Maybe it was. Had I given in to fear, had I not found the courage to leave my family and go with no guarantees of a job, I would not have been on *Jane the Virgin* and would most likely be living with the pain of regret.

Let me be straight up honest with you. There is a guilt we feel under the unspoken pressure of expectations in our intergenerational families of color and immigrant families. It's a fear that holds so many "others" back—the fear of not putting the extended family first. However, I learned that you have to put yourself first. You can't be there for your family if you don't. It's not selfish. It doesn't mean neglecting the people in your life, but in the long run they will benefit too if you take care of you first. I also learned that you have to want your dream more than anyone else around you wants your dream. You must listen compassionately to your own internal dialogue. Your breakthrough is in your mind.

When I returned home to New York, I felt like I was a superhero coming home after an epic battle, like I had been on quest and slayed a dragon. In some sense it was true, because I slayed the dragon of fear. I returned home to my family victorious, exhausted, and filled with pride.

I share the story of how I got the part of Xiomara on *Jane the Virgin* to show you how we, the "others" in life's trenches, hold ourselves back from our destinies. When you boil it down to its true essence, holding ourselves back is just the result of fear. I still hold myself back to this day, but finding the inner power to make one courageous decision against fear leads to the next, and the next, and eventually to what is written in the stars for us. When first we let go of an entrenched fear and take action, it's like being a witch at her cauldron, collaborating with the universe, conjuring and calling things into existence. Manifesting.

I'm not sure how my choices will affect my kids as they grow up, but I think I can safely say that the effect is and will be a positive one. My biggest hope is that observing my choices will give them a model from which to draw upon when it comes time for them to pursue their own big dreams.

The blessings that have come from this one decision continue to blossom. It is not without its challenges. It is really hard sometimes. But it has borne beautiful fruit and continues to bear much more. Just from that one decision to say: "Yes, I will go in spite of my fears."

"It's because you're too soft. You need to toughen up."
~Alba Villanueva
*Jane the Virgin*

# Stand on Your Own Two Feet

Growing up with a single mom in The Bronx, you learn early to stand on your own two feet. Have you ever seen a baby horse being born, how within the first hour it's already standing on its own, building those leg muscles?

Kids in da Bronx, growing up in the city, are like ponies, because for survival there's no time to waste—you better get up, stand up, and start building those instincts for survival. I distinctly remember my first day of kindergarten. My parents had just split. We had moved into my aunt's two-bedroom apartment with her and her three kids. My mom was working for NBC in the check-cashing department, so she couldn't take me herself on my first day of school. Mom was my lifeline and my comfort. I was already feeling like a fish out of water and now my aunt was going to take me to my first day of school. Ugh!

That morning my aunt and I approached the door to the kindergarten classroom. The teacher and students were already there. I felt intimidated when I saw them having fun, already at home in this strange place. How would I fit in?

I noticed that there were lots of toys.

My aunt and the teacher chatted a bit and then my aunt said, "Okay, bye Andrea. I'll pick you up later."

In a panic, I said, "No, don't go!" Even though I wasn't close with her at all, she was all I had at that moment. I didn't want to stay there with all those strangers. She literally had to unhook my skinny little arms that were clinging like vice grips to her leg. Then she quickly vanished. It was so mean! How could she abandon me?

Poof! I was left all alone in this strange place with these strangers. Left to fend for myself, I had no choice but to survive. I spotted some dolls at the back of the room. I took awkward, shaky steps over to them and picked one up. She had blond scraggly hair that looked like a rats' nest, shiny blue eyes, no clothes on, and smudges on her face. She had definitely seen better days. I found a toy brush and began to try to make her look more like a pretty girl and less like a demon child. Then I heard a voice from behind me say, "What's your baby's name?" I turned. It was another little girl, holding a doll of her own. She continued, "Mine is named Cindy."

Oh wow, I thought. This girl seems friendly and she speaks "pretend." I smiled and said, "Mine is called Sarah." In that moment, my nervousness started to dissipate. I knew I was gonna be okay. In about ten minutes, I had become a foal taking her first shaky steps out into this strange new world where mommy was nowhere in sight.

> "Do what you can, with what you have, where you are."
>
> ~Theodore Roosevelt

# Work with What You Got

On the first day we moved from Valentine Avenue to Morris Avenue and Fordham Road, I could hear kids playing in the courtyard of our building entrance. They were boisterously yelling, laughing, having such a good time. I longed to join them, but I was too shy to go out by myself.

Mom was busy unpacking and told me, "Go out and play." I hung back, reluctant, but she said, "Go. And take your new pogo stick."

A pogo stick is a toy for jumping off the ground from a standing position. It's a pole with a spring in the middle, footrests, and handle bars. It was a new toy on The Bronx scene; not many kids had one. In uncomfortable anticipation, I left our apartment and took the pogo stick with me.

I made it to the outside courtyard. All the kids were there. Awkward and shy, I didn't know what to say to them, so I just started jumping on my pogo. With eager fascination the kids turned to me and started in a chorus to ask if they could have a try on the pogo. When I said yes, a fight almost started over who got to go first, second, third, and so on. It was the perfect way to break the ice.

I made fast friends with Sofia and her sister Genesis and I hung out with them the most. I was the kid who could fit in somewhat but not quite. I walked to the beat of my own drum. I was fascinated by many things that most kids my age didn't even notice, like plants and bugs.

Our new home was a one-bedroom apartment on the third floor. It wasn't much but it was all we, a family of four, could afford. Big metal gates covered the bedroom windows from the inside to keep robbers from entering through the fire escape. They opened and closed like an accordion and, if you weren't careful, you might get a finger caught trying to open them. When the gates were open we had the not-so-lovely view of the back of the buildings on the next street. I peered out of the window and saw mostly concrete, with an occasional tree or plant fighting its way through the cracks, looking for sunlight.

Despite the fact that not much was back there, I learned to work with what I had. Curious and self-driven, I loved to explore. I was fascinated with nature, science, and learning about the world around me. I saw the back of my building as a fun place to explore. I would inspect the plants coming through the cracks. Climbing walls, I discovered nooks and crannies where spiders had made a home. One time I found a spider's egg—though at first I didn't know what it was. I was inspecting a spider's web when I noticed a small white cotton-like ball. Fascinated, I pulled it off to get a better look and upon closer inspection I saw the shadow of tiny little black things moving about inside. I needed to know what it was. I attempted to tear the little ball apart. As soon as the tear began to open, out poured streams of baby spiders, leaping like fireworks as they cast their first webs. They looked like tiny paratroopers jumping out of a plane. It was a beautiful sight. My eyes lit up with excitement and surprise as my curiosity was rewarded with a one-of-a-kind experience.

One Christmas, Dad gave me a microscope and dissection kit. It came with real glass to make your own microscope slides, real dissection knives, and a real frog and real crayfish preserved in real formaldehyde! Oh man, they don't make things like that for kids anymore—sharp metal tools, glass, and chemicals. Probably because of one-too-many injuries and lawsuits, but I gotta say that was one cool toy. Yeah, okay, so maybe formaldehyde *has* been linked to cancer and I handled that stuff with my bare hands. Still, that kit sparked my imagination and curiosity. It made real homeschooling happen.

Inspired by Dad's gift, I dreamed of becoming a scientist. I created my own "laboratory" in the corner of our one bedroom. I set up a little desk by the accordion-gated window and neatly organized my microscope and my tools. I kept a pen and notebook handy to jot down notes as I learned about the microscopic world around me. I wanted to find whatever I could to look at under the microscope. I caught roaches in our apartment, dissected them, and created glass slides so I could look at them under my microscope. I spent hours and hours meticulously creating slides and labels: "roach leg," "roach antenna," "fly wing," "spider hair," "Andrea's hair," and even "Andrea's blood"! My blood was hardest to "catch." I had read that a person could see their own blood cells with a microscope by pricking their finger with a needle. "Hey, that's easy!" I thought. "I've got a finger and I've got a needle." Excited, I sat down in my "lab" and proceeded to try to prick my finger for what seemed like forever. I say "tried" because I was so scared of the pain that would come with pricking myself that each time I attempted it, I did it so softly I didn't break the skin enough to make blood come out. (But it still hurt!) Alternately, I would all-together stall, wincing and stopping short, not making contact with my finger at all. This went on for a ridiculous amount of time. I almost gave up. Finally, in a last-ditch effort, because I really, really wanted to see my own blood cells, I took a deep breath, held that needle tightly, raised my hand high, and forcefully brought it down, successfully pricking my finger. I drew a single drop of blood. And damn did that hurt like a mofo! But I did it and was able to make a slide to see my own blood. It was fascinating and *so* worth the pain!

I may not have had a backyard, but that didn't stop me from learning and exploring nature. I may not have had my own room, but I still made my own "science lab" and learned about the scientific world around me. Growing up in The Bronx taught me to work with what I had. It stimulated my curiosity and gave me a thirst to follow my own interests which to this day is still a driving force in my life.

"It's hard to take someone seriously when they leave you a note saying, 'Your ugly.' My ugly what? The idiot didn't even know the difference between your and you're."

~Cara Lynn Shultz

# Speak Well: A Homegirl Grammar Lesson

One of the cool things about living in The Bronx was the Mister Softee ice cream truck. The melody broadcast from the Mister Softee truck sounded like an old-fashioned music box. I found out later it was basically a jangly rendition of "The Farmer in the Dell." The tune was a joyful sound to all of us kids. It made us respond like Pavlov's dog, salivating at the sound as it invoked the thought of eating the creamiest, dreamiest, softest ice cream ever, with rainbow sprinkles, of course, all on top of a delicate crispy wafer cone.

One concrete-hot summer day, all of us kids were playing tag in front of our five-story tenement building on Morris Avenue when in the distance we heard the wonderful jingle of the Mister Softee truck. We all looked in the direction of the music and could see the truck just rounding the corner onto our street. In a mad dash, all the other kids ran to their parents to ask for money to buy ice cream. But I didn't move. My mom was upstairs in our apartment and we hardly ever had money for extras. So I stood there wondering if I should even bother asking her for ice cream money. I watched as all the kids excitedly formed a line and crammed up to the truck. I was feeling so envious. Ugh! I wanted to get ice cream too. Sofia and Genesis came up to me, joyously licking the sprinkles off their ice cream cones. They had an air of entitlement. "Where's your ice cream?" they asked.

I was thinking, "Like everyone has extra money for these things!" but didn't answer.

"You should ask your mom for money," Sofia said. "The truck is leaving soon."

I looked over at the line. There were just three kids left. In seconds, these thoughts raced through my mind: the many times I had to stand there and watch my friends in ecstasy as they ate their Mister Softees; the many times I had asked my mom for ice cream money and she said no. Should I ask again? I weighed my options. The lesser of two evils was the pain of asking for the money and getting a no. To not ask created a definite no. In a panic and to save time I raced through the side alley of our building and yelled for my mom on the third floor. "Moommmyyyy!" I stood waiting for her to pop her head out of the window. Nothing. I yelled again, this time louder. "Mooommmmmmyyyyyyy!" I was so anxious I couldn't stand still. I probably looked like I had to pee. I was nervous that the ice cream truck was gonna leave.

Finally she popped her head out. "Whaatt?!"

"Mommy, Mommy!" I breathlessly said, jumping up and down. "The ice cream truck is here. Can I have some money for ice cream?" I asked with a cheesy smile.

"What?"

I remembered my manners this time when I asked again. "*Please* can I have some money for ice cream?" I then said sweetly, "The ice cream truck is gonna leave!"

Again she replied, but this time a little more intently: "*What*?"

Then the light bulb went on in my head. I knew what she was eluding to. "*May* I please have some money for ice cream?"

A pleased look appeared on her face. "That's better. Just a second." She ducked back into the apartment while I stood there biting my nails, nervously shifting. I was worried the truck was going to leave. Plus, I was annoyed. She took up precious time to make me say "May I." She knew what I meant!

Finally, a sock came flying out of the window with coins in it, as she yelled, "Make sure to bring the sock back home!"

That was one of many homegirl homeschool lessons I got on the spot. Many times Mom would stop me in my tracks and correct my grammar. Her attitude was, "We may not have much, but we're not stupid or uneducated. We will speak well and with our heads held high." Damn, Mom was right. As annoying as it was, I am grateful to her now, as speaking and writing is a huge part of my career. Understanding language and being able to express myself has served me many times over, from being able to read and understand books and scripts, to writing and delivering speeches, to pitching a project idea, and more. Being able to communicate clearly and with intelligence has been a money-making ticket. Thank you, Mom!

> "While it is wise to learn from experience, it is wiser to learn from the experience of others."
>
> ~Rick Warren

# Learn from the Challenges of Others

We lived just off of Fordham Road on Morris Avenue. Fordham Road was a busy main street filled with all kinds of lively businesses: provocative women's clothing retailers, kids' baptismal/communion and *quinceñera* stores, pharmacies, pet shops, and pizzerias. Jerome Avenue was one of the cross streets where you could catch the Number 4 train on the "L" (the elevated subway). Usually parked every few corners on Fordham Road was a guy selling "coquitos." A *coquito* (aka Coco Helado) was freshly made coconut ice cream sold from a pushcart, scooped out and served in a small paper cup. They were a staple dessert in The Bronx, an example of the ingenuity of the immigrant entrepreneurial mindset, which was to work with what you have, work with what you know, and get out there and hustle!

I learned something important walking down Fordham Road one day to buy milk with my mother, who pushed my baby sister Jen in her stroller. As usual, we came upon the *coquito* man with his cart as he rang a cow bell yelling, "Coco Helado! Ven a tomar un delicioso coquito!" Like any normal kid, I asked my mom for one. I can still clearly see the look on her face as she struggled with whether to make me and my sister momentarily happy with a *coquito* or to buy us the milk we needed. She didn't have enough money for both. This was just one of the hard choices she had to make.

Those choices got harder. Back in my day, television sets had antennas called "rabbit ears" that sat on top of a boxy TV. No flat screens back then. Antennas were supposed to boost the signal, but they didn't work 100 percent, so sometimes, to get good reception, you made a contraption from a wire hanger and a strip of aluminum foil. Someone would have to stand there adjusting the makeshift antenna until better reception came through. The dialogue would go something like this:

Antenna holder: "Is it better? Is it better? Is it coming through?"

TV watcher: "No. Move it more to the left."

Antenna holder: "Okay. How about now?"

TV watcher: "No, no, not quite right, try left some more."

They would bend the hanger this way and that and mold the aluminum foil into different shapes, then start again.

TV watcher: "Yes, that's good! Stay there, don't let go!"

Antenna holder: "Hey, I want to watch TV, too!"

At eleven years old, I loved to watch TV. The "it" girl at the time was Brooke Shields. She caused a sensation in the famous Calvin Klein jeans ad: "Nothing gets between me and my Calvins." As designer jeans started to gain traction with consumers, everyone, including my friends, started to sport them. I had never been concerned with what I wore, or what I looked like, until I was approaching my tween years when the seductive fifteen-year-old Brooke Shields appeared on my rabbit-eared TV promoting Calvin Klein jeans. Those jeans were very expensive, just as they are to this day.

Young and impressionable, looking at Brooke, I lived vicariously through her. I thought, "My god, she's so beautiful. I want to be her. I want to do the things she's doing. I want to be a model. I want to be an actress." Brooke touted the jeans using lines that had a great impact on me, my classmates, and neighbors. Quotes like these became part of our psyche:

"Whenever I get some money I buy Calvins, and if there's any left, I pay the rent."

"You wanna know what comes between me and my Calvins? Nothing."

My friends would show off their new designer jeans with an air of entitlement and normalcy like it was nothing to buy a pair. I felt the monetary limitations that my friends Sofia and Genesis didn't seem to have, even though their mom was on welfare too. Their mom's boyfriend apparently had money and was always buying them stuff.

I desperately wanted to fit in with my friends, so I begged my mother for a pair of designer jeans. To buy me a *coquito* was a major financial decision, so of course, her answer was, "No, we can't afford them."

That September, we went school clothes shopping. She took to me to Alexanders department store on the corner of Fordham Road and Grand Concourse and got me a pair of no-name brand jeans. Ugh! I felt like such a dork in them. They looked nothing like the cool jeans my friends were wearing. They were stiff, had a rough texture, bell-bottom legs, and a waist so high they almost came up to my chest. Plus my skinny ass had no beef, which the jeans really accentuated.

That Christmas, I begged my mom again for designer jeans, although I knew it was next to impossible that she could get them for me. Despite not having much money, somehow we always had a lot of presents under the tree and that Christmas was no different. To my surprise, I opened a gift from "Santa" and inside were a pair of Jordache jeans! Jordache was as popular, if not more so, as Calvins. But how, Santa Mom, did you pull this off?

Oh Lordy, was I so excited. I couldn't wait to put them on. From that point on, I only wore my Jordache jeans. I refused to wear the dorky Alexander department store ones. I finally felt like I fit in, sorta. I was still an introvert, awkward, and somewhat dorky. I wore my Jordaches for countless days. I refused to wash them because then I would have had to resort to wearing the dorky no-name brand ones while the Jordaches were in the wash. That thought left me mortified.

Nevertheless, one day, I finally had to cave in when my Jordaches starting to stand up by themselves!

As I look back, I am grateful for the *coquito* and Calvins experiences because they motivated me. I never wanted to be in the position of having to make such hard money choices and Mom's choices taught me that the basic *needs*—milk, rent—came first, before *wants*. Making sure I don't repeat those experiences, those feelings have fueled my life and my career. If I had had everything, I would not have learned what it meant to be hungry—literally and figuratively. I would not have learned to be grateful. Plus, in that gift, the Jordache jeans, my mother taught me that her love for me does not waiver. She may not always have had the means to provide extras, but she showed up for me, time and time again, in unexpected ways. Motivated by love she came through, bearing gifts. The most important was her love. I will forever be grateful for the love she showed by gifting me what I knew we couldn't afford, but which she knew would affirm me.

"She needed a hero, so that's what she became."
~Narrator
*Jane the Virgin*

# Be Your Own Damn Hero

Growing up in The Bronx *was* challenging. We were surrounded by poverty, drug use, and concrete. In the 1970s the US economy was in a recession for several years and New York City was hit particularly hard, especially minority communities. The blackout of 1977 made matters even worse. Crime was high and jobs were scarce. However, what the media neglected to notice was that there were human beings living in these areas, including me and my family.

Films, books, and media like *The Taking of Pelham 123* or *Fort Apache, The Bronx* or *The Bonfire of the Vanities* have identified the horrors of The Bronx. Some critics complained that the South Bronx of *Bonfire* was a caricature that made a bad situation worse. In fact, the book provoked protests from Bronx boosters.

> "To be honest, I never bought the premise of 'Bonfire,'" Professor Chinn said. "Rather, it was a symbol of terrifying otherness, … The Bronx of 'Bonfire' is the Bronx of the white imagination, not the Bronx of, say, DJ Kool Herc or, not to press the point, Sonia Sotomayor."
>
> To which Mr. Ferrer added: "That's why they call it fiction."
> ~Sam Roberts, *New York Times,* December 9, 2012
> (https://archive.nytimes.com/cityroom.blogs.nytimes.com
> /2012/12/09/bonfire-by-roberts/)

Mom had always worked and made her own money, but she lost her way for a bit. It wasn't easy to get by or make ends meet. We eventually ended up having to go on welfare for a couple of years. I remember the shame and embarrassment Mom experienced at the welfare office when we went to apply. She was treated like a third-class citizen. The workers seemed to look down on her for being there, as if she was lazy and begging for a handout. That was the moment I realized we were poor and first experienced the feeling of being "less than" and the "other."

One of things they gave you at the welfare office was food stamps, coupons that you could only use in the supermarket to buy food. No cash was given. Food stamps could only be spent on necessities, not drugs or alcohol. Standing in the checkout line in the supermarket, even the minimum-wage cashier looked down on us when my mother handed her the coupons. My mother's shame became my shame.

Another subsidy the government provided the poor was cheese, aka "government cheese" or "welfare cheese." In 1981 the US produced too much cheese—1.4 billion pounds of it. To provide support to dairy farmers, the US Government ended up with a ridiculous surplus of dairy, and President Ronald Reagan in not so many words declared, "Let them eat cheese!" and had 30 million pounds of it distributed to food pantries and other welfare programs. Welfare cheese was a Day-Glo orange, five-pound block. One had to wait in a long line in order to get it. It did make for a mean grilled-cheese sandwich, I gotta say. Work with whatchu got, right?

Mom had a lot to deal with: a toxic marriage, no job, no money, two kids, and not a lot of options. Fortunately she decided to take brave steps toward making a change. Mom enrolled in a job training program through the Puerto Rican Family Institute. She took classes during the day, came home and did homework at night. She was determined not to be a victim of circumstance, to get herself back into the workforce and all of us off of welfare. After nine months she completed the program and got a full-time job working in downtown Manhattan on Wall Street, for Merrill Lynch in the original World Trade Center. She then left the bad marriage and found another place for us to live.

Witnessing my mother's struggles had a big impact on me. Witnessing her pick herself up and make a change for the better had an even bigger impact. She improved all our lives. Those brave, difficult actions she took were so worth it. Her actions, to this day, are still having positive effects on my life and even on the lives of my children.

There's something to be said about not having. It can make you hungry, motivated, and fuel you toward success. I learned from my mother that I can do hard things. If Mom can do it, so can I. She taught by example that if you're not happy with where you're at, do something about it. Don't just sit there and complain or throw your hands up and say, "I can't, woe is me." Decide what it is you want or need and then take action! Be your own damn hero. Yes, it might be hard to make major changes and improve your life situation, but with repeated action over time those changes will happen. One day you will look back and be amazed at how far you've come. I am forever grateful to her for being a shining example of bravery, self-empowerment, courage, and hard work—my shero.

# Play Hooky: The Bennies of a Homegirl Field Trip

I wasn't the best student. There wasn't much guidance. I was
just expected to do well. I would show up to school but I had
no idea I was supposed to focus, listen, and pay attention as
well. Now, as I look back, I can see that my mind was all over
the place. I probably would've been diagnosed with Inatten-
tive ADHD. School was mostly boring, with the occasional
fun thing like learning how to sew a skirt for our grammar school graduation or any kind of project that involved
hands-on learning. In the fifth grade, aged ten, we had to
learn all of the fifty states of the USA. That was completely
overwhelming to me, and boring. How do you get all of those
arbitrary names into your head and for what reason? It was

beyond me until my teacher gave me an assignment to create a map of the US by coloring each state with food-colored rice grains and glue! Now we're talking, Mr. Stanley. I absolutely loved that project. Another hands-on project I remember was creating a model of an Egyptian pyramid out of plaster. We had been learning about the Egyptians and were assigned the task of making a model from that time period. I loved clay and Play-Doh so this was perfect. I was so excited by this. I even went all by myself to the hardware store to buy the plaster for the project.

From time to time, Dad would take me on a weekend day trip to see theater or visit a museum. My favorite was the Metropolitan Museum of Art, especially the Egyptian exhibit with the mummies and the artifacts made of gold. My other favorites were the rooms decorated in the styles of the 1700s and 1800s and the costumes of that era as well. I would imagine myself living in that time period in rooms and clothes like those. They seemed so rich and decadent. I thought you had to be a very happy person to live like that.

As I said, I wasn't the best student. One day the teacher sent me home with a letter to give to my mother. I handed it to her and she read it. Apparently, it said I was behind in reading and needed to get better or they would not move me up to the next grade. Oh snap! Mom didn't look too happy. What made matters worse was that my cousin Katrina, who was my age, was a straight-A student and an avid reader. Every time our family got together, her nose was in a book. We would hear all about how well she was doing in school and how she was excelling in her ballet class. I couldn't help but feel compared to her.

My aunt, Titi Lola, Katrina's mother, suggested to my mom that it would help me if I read for one hour a day. Mom took her advice and from then on, almost every day, she would call me to read, interrupting my playtime. I hated it. She would send me into our one bedroom, hand me a book and say, "Read. I will let you know when the time is up." It's not fun to be told what to do or to be forced to do something that you don't want to do. So I would sit there and rebelliously not read. Every so often Mom would open the door and check to see if I was indeed reading and I would scramble to pick the book up and pretend like I was. She would give me the evil eye, knowing what I was up to, and threaten to extend my reading time. Little did I know I was cheating myself. Eventually, bored with doing nothing, I would pick up the book and begrudgingly read.

After a while I started to get into the books I was trying not to read. I'll never forget one of my favorites: *From the Mixed-Up Files of Mrs. Basil E. Frankweiler* by E. L. Konigsburg. OMG! What a fun story. It took place in my favorite museum, the Met, and in some of my favorite exhibits. That was the first book I connected with. From it, I experienced the joy of virtual travel. I lived vicariously through the main characters, Claudia and Jamie Kincaid, as they ran away from home to live in the Metropolitan Museum of Art in New York City. They would hide in the restroom at closing time, as security staff checked to see that all the patrons had departed; blend in with school groups on tour; bathe in the fountain; use "wishing coins" for money; and sleep in an antique bed. I knew that exact bed and had dreamt of sleeping in it the first time I saw it on one of my visits to the Met!

That book is a standout for me as I look back on my childhood. I enjoyed it so much that, years later when I was in high school, I played hooky twice to go to the Met by myself.

What was great about the Met was that you didn't have to pay an entrance fee, just a donation. I had no money so I never made a donation—which I felt guilty about—but that didn't stop me. I would wander the museum for hours. I spent most of my time either in the costumes area with all of the beautiful gowns or in the section of furnished rooms from historic time periods, especially my favorite eras of the 1700s and 1800s. I envisioned myself as a rich lady dressed in extravagant gowns, waking up in an elegant four-postered canopy bed, covered with satin and velvet linens. The great film *Amadeus*, about the classical musician Mozart, further fed my fantasies about that time period and I started to listen to classical music. Mozart was my favorite and I "borrowed" a record from the school library. I never returned it though. I loved it so much, I didn't want to give it up.

Growing up in The Bronx I learned to work with what I had. What did I have? Only one of the greatest museums in the world! All kids, including those from the hood, have an innate intelligence and curiosity. The chance to follow their interests can lead to lots of learning and create a natural career path.

Hooky Field Trips taught me to think independently, plan, and follow through. A bridge-and-tunnel kid, I learned how to bravely get to Manhattan and navigate the subway by myself. If I had just gone to school like I was supposed to, I would never have experienced the wonder and benefits of my own "field trips." I went from just reading about art and music to exposure to them. Those of us from The Bronx know the benefits of not conforming, the value of sometimes breaking the rules.

"Now it's your turn to listen to me, because I know how to take care of sixteen-year-old bitches."
~Xiomara Villanueva
*Jane the Virgin*

# Sometimes You Just Gotta Go Bronx

My dad grew up on the mean streets of NYC. He had his share of the school of hard knocks. He was a tough dude. He had to be. But he was also smart. He loved learning and believed in the arts and higher education. He was a walking contradiction because he was exposed to higher learning in prison. He did a one-year stint at the infamous Rikers. I still don't know why he went to jail. He won't tell me. It's clear that he's not proud of it, though he likes to joke that he graduated from "Rikers U" because he left prison with a high school diploma. I am so grateful to my dad for being a living example. He demonstrated that one can make big mistakes in life but one can also decide to make a change for the better. I am also grateful for his passion for learning. He exposed me to so much, like art, science, and the importance of higher learning. Without that exposure, I wouldn't be where I am today.

One of the things he exposed me to was self-defense, not being a victim. I was a meek, shy, quiet, skinny kid. I didn't like confrontation (and to this day still don't), but I had to learn the hard way because, growing up in The Bronx, that's just not gonna fly. I was gonna have to toughen up or get eaten alive.

Dad could see that I was a softy and was concerned for me. He saw my timidity and wanted to arm me with confidence and teach me how to protect myself. So he enrolled me in a tae kwon do school. He was going to college full time to study nursing and was working full time as a medical technician. My parents had long split—when I was five years old—and the only housing my father could afford was a rented room in someone's house. Finding money in his tight budget to send me to a martial arts school was a big deal. It showed he loved me and wanted to make sure that I could protect myself.

At the time Bruce Lee was all the rage. Karate films were super popular and the song "Everybody Was Kung Fu Fighting" was on constant replay on radio airwaves. Karate had a super-human mystique. The idea that you could use your body to make an attacker go flying was so cool.

I was nine years old when Dad enrolled me in Master Hwang's School of Tae Kwon Do. The inside of the school was covered in 1970s brown-and-tan wood paneling, mirrors, and awards. In the main hallway was a huge picture of Master Hwang performing a split high-kick and just below it hung a quote: "I come to you in peace and brotherhood for I have no weapons. But should I be forced to defend myself, my principles, or my honor; should it be a matter of right or wrong; then here are my weapons—my empty hands and feet."

Tae kwon do was challenging, but was just what I needed. I attended class twice a week. The owner of the school, Master Hwang, was tough. A task master, he ruled the school with an iron fist and kept us kids in line as he pushed us toward mastery and discipline.

Instruction would start with all us students lining up and walking into the classroom based on belt rank. Next, we said our student oath:

I shall observe the tenets of tae kwon do
I shall respect the instructor and seniors
I shall never misuse tae kwon do
I shall be a champion of freedom and justice
I shall build a more peaceful world

We would then begin our stretching routine followed by calisthenics, push-ups, sit-ups, punching, and kicking drills. Then we learned and practiced formal techniques in punching, blocking, and kicking, along with forms—a sparring choreography with prearranged punches, blocks, and kicks;

maneuvers to respond to an attack. It was super challenging for me but it was fun. I was able to learn the forms somewhat easily and my coordination was pretty good, but whenever I had to demonstrate a form in front of people I always looked down. I was timid in the face of scrutiny by my instructors and fellow classmates.

Besides practicing our punches and kicks a gazillion times we also did lots of stretching. It was a big deal if someone could do a split; that seemed to be the goal everyone was reaching for.

I attended Master Hwang's for an entire school year, then went on summer break. After break, I returned. On my first day back to tae kwon do class, as always, we started with a stretching routine. When it was time for our open leg stretch, to my amazement I fell easily into a full split! Everyone in class turned and looked at me, impressed and surprised. I was just as surprised as they were. I had no idea that I could do a split! Over summer break I didn't practice stretching at all. Nor did I practice any tae kwon do techniques. But I wasn't gonna let them know that, so I played it off. "Oh, yeah, I do the splits," I said casually, impressed with myself as I continued stretching into my newfound flexibility with a confidence I had never known.

What an awesome lesson to learn firsthand, that there is a compound effect that comes with repetition and practice over a significant amount of time. With enough time, results show—even after a break. My muscles were practiced and got to take a rest over the summer. Eventually they relaxed into the direction I had been trying to make them go. Now that I could do the splits, my kicks were graceful, high, and effective. I was really starting to look like a martial artist.

Despite my newfound leg-splitting ability, I was still meek, shy, and as skinny as can be. No meat on my bones. Kids would taunt me: "Hey bag of bones!" or "Flaca!" which means skinny in Spanish, or "Where's the beef?" *à la* the famous Wendy's commercial. It was embarrassing! Most kids in my neighborhood had "beef" on their bones. Ugh, I really wanted some beef too! I wanted to fit in. While Mom reassured me that I was perfect the way I was, Dad's response was to keep me enrolled in martial arts to toughen me up.

At the time *Wonder Woman* was really popular on TV. I loved that show. That a woman could be strong and tough was so cool. I was inspired by the idea of being in control, able to kick some ass, and all the while still look pretty, with not a hair out of place. During commercial breaks Underoos, kids underwear produced by the Fruit of the Loom company, was advertised. The commercials featured characters from popular entertainment, especially comic superheroes. Their tag line was "Underwear that's fun to wear." I wanted to have fun wearing my underwear too! I begged my mom to get me some, but money was tight. However, one day Mom came through—like she always did—and brought home superhero undies. I was slightly disappointed when I saw that they were knockoffs, not as cool as the brand name, but I quickly got over it, grateful to Mom for coming through like that, happy with what I could get.

The next day I was excited to sport my new undies at tae kwon do class. As I got my clothes ready for the day, I laid out all three pairs of the Underoo knock-offs on my bed. I stood for a while contemplating the all-important decision of which pair to wear to tae kwon do: Batgirl, Supergirl, or Wonder Woman. Hmmm! Decisions, decisions, decisions. I weighed my options, trying to pick the right pair for the job. Batgirl had been trained for peak physical fitness including great speed, flexibility, and strength, but sadly she had no supernatural powers. Supergirl, on the other hand, could fly, possessed super-strength, and had psychokinetic, shapeshifting, and cloaking/invisibility powers that made her undetectable, even to Superman! And last, but not least, was Wonder Woman! Wonder Woman's powers were drawn from certain traits of the Greek goddesses who created her. Her physical feats were impressive, with superior strength, flight, stamina, speed, and agility that allowed her to easily overpower foes with nothing but her godlike strength. Wonder Woman also wore a tiara (What little girl doesn't love a tiara?) that doubled as a boomerang-like weapon, had beautiful gold bracelets that could deflect bullets, and wielded the golden Lasso of Truth! Plus, she was trained in hand-to-hand combat similar to tae kwon do! She was loving, just, kind, and freakin' gorgeous, with a slammin' body. As much as I loved Batgirl and Supergirl, Wonder Woman was the clear standout. Decision made! Wonder Woman Underoos it was.

Feeling good, and with a little extra pep in my step, I made it to Master Hwang's. Some students were already in the changing room, including the two sisters I will now call Anastasia and Drizella. Anastasia was sixteen and Drizella was seventeen. I looked up to them—teenagers, I thought they were so cool. They seemed so grown up. They wore pretty makeup and trendy clothes. Their air of confidence seemed unattainable. As I undressed in the cramped changing room, when I got down to my undies all of a sudden Anastasia and Drizella start laughing and pointing to my underwear. In baby voices, they snickered, "Oh Andrea, are you wearing your wittle superhero panties? How old are you—five?" Everyone in the room looked at me and laughed.

Instantly, my Wonder Woman undies weren't so wonderful. The heat of embarrassment and shame washed over my face. I thought to myself, "How did I miss this? Are they right? Am I too old to be into superheroes and wear Underoos? Am I dumb or something?" I didn't know how to respond. The evil sisters picked up on my shame and decided to capitalize on it. From that day on whenever we were in the changing room they would tease and make fun of me in front of the others. They seemed to experience such joy in ridiculing me. I had no idea how to handle the situation or how to get them stop.

I was so full of shame and fear that I kept the bullying a secret for months. No one except the girls in my tae kwon do class knew what was happening. However, that changed when the verbal torture got physical. One day after class, as always,

I raced into the changing room. I wanted to get dressed as fast as I could, so that I didn't have to be in the changing room for too long, to minimize my exposure to the evil sisters. But as soon as Anastasia and Drizella made it into the changing room, they started in on me. Annoyed, I quickly picked up my bag, ready to walk out. Unfortunately, I had to walk by them. Anastasia, the sixteen-year-old, said, "Bye. See you next time, stupid," and stuck her foot out, making me trip and fall. They both laughed as Anastasia said, "Hey, stupid! You walked into my foot. You better watch where you're walking next time."

As usual, shame and embarrassment came over me, but this time accompanied by a fear that I hadn't experienced before. I felt threatened. It felt like their treatment was getting worse. I thought they were going to hurt me.

I ran home crying and my mother asked, "What's the matter? What happened?" In an uncontrollable, blubbering mess, I told Mom everything. I couldn't hold it in anymore. As she listened, her face went from worry to a grim steely look of determination. She looked me in my eyes and said, "Don't worry. Mommy will take care of it. When is your next class?"

Sobbing, I said, "Saturday."

"Okay, I am going with you on Saturday." And then she walked away.

Uh-oh! Fudge! What the heck is going to happen? When Mom gets angry, she is no joke. There was no telling what she would do.

Well, Saturday morning rolled around in the blink of an eye. It was the middle of January. We had had lots and lots of snow. As usual, funds were tight. My little sister Jennifer was about three years old. All we could afford was an umbrella stroller for her, which is ultra-lightweight, basic, and folds down to be about the size of a—you guessed it—umbrella. It's often a secondary stroller for when you need to travel light. But this was no secondary stroller for us. It was the only one we had. All bundled up, we trudged our way through the snow-filled streets to Master Hwang's School of Tae Kwon Do.

Mom was pissed. The look on her face was stern. Her lips were in a tightly pursed line as she pushed that flimsy umbrella stroller with my sister strapped in tight. Mounds of snow and ice only added fuel to Mom's fire. I could feel the heat of her anger rise as the minutes passed. While she fought her way through the ice and snow, pushing that flimsy umbrella stroller, all of a sudden one of the wheels broke off. Oh snap! OMG! I could practically see fire coming out of Mom's ears. Now she had to push little Jennifer in a three-wheeled crappy stroller.

When we finally made it to the school, Mom asked me to point out the evil sisters. I pointed to them and she asked, "Which is the one that tripped you?" I pointed to Anastasia. She said, "Okay, go into class." As class started my mother sat with arms crossed and demon eyes. She stared at the sisters for the entire hourlong class. Wouldn't take her eyes off of them.

At the end of class we filed out in a line into the hallway. My mother was there, waiting. She went up to Anastasia and said, "Hey, I wanna talk to you. Did you trip my daughter?"

"What?" Anastasia was confused.

"I *said*, did you trip my daughter?"

From behind Anastasia came her older sister Drizella, who got in my mother's face and said, "You got a problem with my sister, you got a problem with me."

"Oh yeah?" said my mother, and without batting an eyelash she punched Drizella in the face. All hell broke loose. Mom and Drizella were fighting. It was so upsetting, I started to cry, worried that my mother was going to get hurt. Then Mom's glasses went flying. Not good. They were welfare-issued glasses. Welfare-issued glasses were not the best quality and you only received one pair. If you lost or broke them, you were shit out of luck. You'd have to sacrifice one of your kids in order to afford another pair.

Finally Master Hwang and his instructors came running in and broke up the fight. "What the hell is going on? Please calm down. What happened?"

"Those two have been bullying my daughter," my mother yelled.

He took my mom into his office, closing the door.

Anastasia and Drizella started crying, trying to act innocent and get everyone's sympathy. They yelled at me, "This is all your fault!"

My tears stopped as anger started to rise in me. "My fault?" I thought "How is this *my* fault?" Then a bravery I had never experienced came out of nowhere. I yelled, using a real curse word for the first time in my life—"You fuckin' liars!"—as I lunged, trying to kick Drizella. I wasn't afraid anymore. It was one thing to let someone bully me, but it was a whole other thing for someone to hurt Mom. I loved her. I would've killed for her. Fortunately for me, someone held me back. Not sure what I would've done anyway.

Finally Master Hwang called us into his office. He listened to my side of the story and then the evil sisters' side. Once it was all out, Master Hwang chastised my mother: "This is no way to handle this. Why didn't you come to me first? We're trying to teach these kids to use fighting in a disciplined manner."

"Forget discipline. No one messes with my kids!" she said. "I want to talk to their parents."

"Oh no, please don't call our parents, please!" Drizella and Anastasia said in a panic. "Our parents are gonna kill us!"

"Good. You need to learn a lesson," Mom said. "How old are you? Sixteen and seventeen and you're picking on a nine-year-old? No, I want to talk to your parents."

"No, please don't call our parents."

"And what about my glasses? They're broken! I only get one pair of glasses. Somebody's gonna pay to replace them. These cost $110!"

Master Hwang asked, "What if the girls paid you a little bit every week to replace them? Would you hold off on calling their parents?"

Mom wasn't sure.

The girls were like, "Yes, we'll do whatever, but please don't tell our parents."

"Okay," Mom said. "Every week you have to give my daughter at least $2 until you completely pay the cost of replacing my glasses. If you don't pay it off completely, I *will* call your parents."

And that's just what they did. Every week thereafter Drizella and Anastasia would pay me the money and were as sweet as pie to me. They would even try to give me candy, but I never let my guard down. I said nothing to them, just took the money without even giving them a smile. Finally, months later they gave me the last and final payment for Mom's glasses. Now that's what I'm talking about! Street justice in its pure form. Mom had to go Bronx. She used her hands and feet to defend my honor and taught those girls a lesson. Pick on someone your own size and don't mess with my kids! Go Mom!

Mom told me that violence shouldn't be the only way to solve a problem, but sometimes you just have to go Bronx on someone. Sometimes it's the only thing that will work and get respect. She told me several times, "Somebody hits you, hit right back!" and eventually I had to go Bronx too; well, sort of.

One morning back at my grammar school, PS 33, I had apparently bumped into this girl by mistake as we were filing into class. Her name was Kendra. She got pissed and gave me some words. I didn't like confrontation and tried to get her to leave me alone by ignoring her, but she kept trying to get me to argue with her. The other students watched. It was awkward. I wasn't sure what to do. Thankfully the teacher came into the classroom and told everyone to sit down. Relieved, I thought that was the last of it, but later on someone quietly slipped me a note. I opened it. It was from Kendra. It said she was gonna kick my ass after school. Oh my god! My heart started racing. I felt butterflies in my tummy. I didn't know how to fight. I had only been in tae kwon do school for six months. I had never had a real fight before and now Kendra was gonna kick my ass! A feeling of dread settled into my entire being. I couldn't pay attention at all in class. All I could think was, "What the heck am I gonna do? Maybe I could sneak out?"

When the final bell rang, I tried my best to pack up my stuff quickly and walk out of the building as fast as I could. I made it to the front of the school and thought I was in the clear when out of nowhere Kendra called my name, ran up to me, and got in my face: "We are gonna fight!" Kids gathered in a crowd around us and started jeering us on. She threw her book bag down and rolled up her sleeves and started to posture to me. I froze with fear. She pushed my shoulder to egg me on to fight. I didn't know what to do. Then she approached me again and, without thinking, I gave her a front kick to the stomach and she literally went flying, just like the movies, and landed on her butt!

The crowd went, "Ooooohhhh snap!"

She was dumbfounded. Honestly, I was in shock too! I must've practiced that front kick hundreds of times. I had no idea it would work, no idea it was so powerful. It scared the shit out of me. I didn't know I could do that! It kinda felt good though.

Kendra scrambled to her feet. I could tell she was embarrassed and she was even more pissed than before. I didn't know what my next move was gonna be. I was scared and uncomfortable. I just wanted my mom. As she started toward me, I quickly picked up my bag and ran. The kids laughed while Kendra yelled for me to come back to fight, calling me a chicken.

When I finally got home, I was crying and my mom worriedly asked me what had happened. I explained the whole situation. She took me in her arms to comfort me and said, "It's okay baby," and looked me in my eyes and said, "Good for you. Don't ever let someone hit you. You hit them right back!"

Okay, so it wasn't exactly going Bronx. In reality, I accidentally defended myself. However, all of those hundreds of kicks I had to practice in tae kwon do class actually came in handy. I learned firsthand how effective they were. And even though I ran away, I experienced what it was to take action and defend myself, which came in handy years later.

"End of Story. Well you know what, I'm the writer. I'll end the story"

~Jane Gloriana Villanueva
*Jane the Virgin*

# Draw the Line

We moved from Morris Avenue and Fordham Road to the Hunts Point/Fort Apache section of the South Bronx after my mom left a toxic second marriage. It was a brand-new start for the three of us: Mom, my little sister, and me.

Our new neighborhood looked like a war zone though. Lots of burned out or demolished buildings. The value in the buildings had been plummeting so, in order to recoup their money, landlords committed a lot of arson. Hence the phrase, "The Bronx is burning."

It wasn't easy getting used to this neighborhood. Behind our new building and next to it were abandoned buildings which were crumbling into rubble. We got to move into a two-bedroom apartment in one of the newly rehabbed buildings in the area. It was pretty cool to move into a brand-new place, but the trade-off was it was on the other side of The Bronx, far from my friends.

A tween, my body was changing. Overnight it seemed like I woke up with boobs! Always really skinny, now I was skinny with boobs. Walking down the street past guys hanging out in front of the corner bodega or construction guys taking a break for a smoke was like going on a psychological roller coaster. I could feel their stares bore into me. More often than not those stares were followed by words that repulsed me. "Hey mamacita, why you so sad? Let's see you smile." Or, "Mmmm damn, I want me somadat." Uncomfortable with this new body and the attention it garnered, I would wear baggy shirts to hide myself. I didn't know what to do with my boobs. I experienced a sense of insecurity I had never known before, compounded by having to attend a different middle school, IS 74. I could take the bus part-way, but I still had a long walk. I walked by myself at 7:30 in the morning past drug dealers, homeless guys, and prostitutes, under the overpass of the Bruckner Expressway. Many winter days I froze my ass off, but mostly because I didn't dress properly for the weather. I didn't want to wear a hat; it would mess up my hair!

A new school isn't easy for any kid, but it is even harder living in the South Bronx, not the nice part of town. I didn't make friends easily. I was awkward, not one of the cool kids, didn't wear designer clothes, wasn't popular or able to make cool come-backs when teased. I didn't fit in and felt like an outsider. I had always been somewhat timid in new situations or with people I didn't know. I wasn't completely shy. I could be outgoing and funny with my friends, but now all the friends I had were back on Morris Avenue, on the other side of The Bronx. I was in my tweens, one of the most difficult stages of a girl's life, starting a new school in a new neighborhood, with no friends. I didn't know how to talk to people or approach them. So as the school year went on, I kept my head down most of the time and tried to keep to myself.

One day in the cafeteria a group of girls was talking and laughing. I watched them, wishing I could be part of a group. One of the girls seemed to be in charge. Her name was Willa. Surprisingly she had a thin build like me, but unlike me she was scrappy and had a mean face. You could tell that she was tough. All of a sudden, she looked at me and asked, "What the f*** are you looking at?" Gulp. I didn't realize I had been staring. I didn't know what to say. She saw my timidity and her eyes seemed to smile. I looked away. That was the beginning of the torture. For the rest of the school year she tormented me, verbally intimidated me, and made fun of me in front of others. I was so scared of her.

After months, Willa hadn't let up. I was so unhappy at school. I wanted the torture to stop. I decided out of desperation to tell my mom what had been happening. I feared how Mom would react, especially after that tae kwon do fiasco years back, but I was more scared of Willa. I was desperate and really couldn't take it anymore. Through a flood of tears,

I told Mom everything. Mom listened compassionately and, with that all-too-familiar look of anger, said, "Okay, I am going with you to school tomorrow and we are talking with the principal."

"Oh snap! I hope she doesn't punch the principal out," I thought.

The next day we were in the principal's office and my mother sternly but calmly explained to him what had been happening, then asked, "What are you gonna do about this?" The principal sat there for a few seconds, threw his hands up, and said, "There's not much I can do. We'd have to catch her in the act. It's Andrea's word against hers," and he basically washed his hands of it. Mom looked at him, her face contorting like Linda Blair in *The Exorcist* as disbelief turned to anger. Man oh man, if looks could kill, Mr. Jones would've fallen out of his chair and landed on the floor in a dead heap. With demon eyes, Mom turned to me and through gritted teeth said, "Andrea, I am telling you right now in front of the principal" (as she pointed to him), "that if that girl hits you, I am giving you permission to hit her back! Do you understand me? If that girl lays a finger on you, I am giving you permission to hit her back." Then she faced the principal, still pointing her finger at him, and said, "And you better not suspend my daughter. Because we came to you for help and you're saying you're not gonna do anything? She has every right to defend herself and she will not be suspended for it!" Damn Mom! Lay down the law!

Not too long after that day I got sick with a cold and had a fever for a couple of days, a perfect excuse not to go to school. Finally, after three days of staying home, Mom said I had to go back. I played like I still wasn't feeling well enough, but she was on to me, and so I schlepped in the freezing cold past the homeless people, drug dealers, and local prostitutes and made it to school early. Exhausted, I leaned against the wall outside of my classroom waiting for the teacher and other students to show up. I wasn't feeling great and was in a foul mood. I had just gotten my period that morning and was still weak from being sick. Then, in the near distance, down the hall, I heard voices. I looked up and, as luck would have it, Willa and one of her cronies were walking my way. When Willa spotted me, she smiled a surly smile. "Oh shit!" I thought. "I'm not in the mood. I am so fucking tired of her! I'm not gonna take her shit anymore." I didn't know what I was going to do, but I knew I was done.

Willa sauntered up to me. "Hi Andrea." I rolled my eyes and turned my head away without a response. "Hey! I'm talking to you," she said. "You don't say 'Hi' to your friend?"

"I'm not your friend."

"Yes, you are," she said in a threatening tone. "You *are* my friend." She leaned up against the wall next to me and menacingly whispered in my ear, "You're my friend, right?"

Nervous, but really, really angry and tired, I responded, "No, I'm not your friend."

She then put her arm around my shoulders and asked again, even more threateningly, "You're my friend, right?"

And then a switch flipped in my brain. I swung my arm and elbowed her in the stomach. Next thing I knew we were in a ball, fighting on the floor. Other kids arriving at school ran up to watch us, shouting "Kick her ass!" And yes, Willa was indeed kicking my ass. She was on top of me, scratching the shit out of my face. I couldn't get her off of me. I tried to stop her, punching and scratching back, which felt kinda good, but unfortunately I was not very effective. Finally some teachers arrived and pulled Willa off of me.

We were both sent to the principal's office. I told my version of the story. Then she told hers, which was that I had started the fight. We were both sent home.

I aggressively strode home, passing the same homeless guys and drug dealers. The prostitutes were gone though. (Had to get some rest for the next shift?) My body was aching. The scratches on my face were burning as tears streamed down my face. I was so angry. And so embarrassed.

When Mom got home from work, I told her what happened. She then called my father. He came over right away. When Dad saw my scratched-up face he was so upset. He said, "That's it! I'm taking you to school tomorrow. We are going to speak to the principal." The next day, as my Dad and I walked into the building, a lot of kids turned to look at us. One of the kids was Willa. The kids murmured and whispered: "Oh shit. Her dad's a cop." My father is Puerto Rican, but he's got light brown hair, white skin, and blue eyes. So to most people he "looks" white, which is why they thought he was a cop. Willa looked scared. A small smile came over my face and I walked a little taller, thinking to myself, "Yeah, that's right Willa, it's your turn to be scared."

In the principal's office, my father asked him what he was going to do about the situation and the principal said, "I'm going to suspend Willa, but Andrea will not be suspended."

Yes! Vindication.

Willa never bothered me again and even tried to be my friend. I learned how to stand up for myself that day. I may not have looked like a cool martial artist in the movies, but I put an end to that story. I experienced a feeling of personal strength, a sense of self-worth and agency. I thought, "I don't have to take being mistreated. I can do something about it." I was never bullied again.

"A person without the knowledge of their past history, origin, and culture is like a tree without roots."

~Marcus Garvey

# Discover Your Roots

My mother grew up in the United States in the 1950s and 1960s, which wasn't a time of Puerto Rican flag waving and cultural pride like we're experiencing now. It was just the opposite. She was told that she was a greasy dirty spic. Speaking Spanish outside of the home was an embarrassment. Assimilating into American culture was the goal. I'm sure many of you have family with similar experiences and know what I am talking about.

I grew up in a mostly Black and Latino neighborhood. I knew that I was Puerto Rican but didn't know what that meant. Puerto Rico was a far-off island in someplace called the Caribbean where they spoke Spanish. I had a grandmother who lived there, Grandma Benny, but I never saw her.

My other grandmother, my mother's mother, Grandma Iris, spoke Spanish, but she also spoke English with an accent. My mom mostly spoke in English, but when she got frustrated she was very fluent in Spanish curse words. We ate Puerto Rican food on Sundays when we visited Grandma Iris. It was at her house where we usually had "house parties." Back then a house party was a spontaneous slapped-together gathering of family and friends. Nothing fancy, just lots of home-cooked food, wine, beer, and music playing on the record player. Lots of dancing, laughing, drinking, and smoking. It was the 1970s and salsa music was all the rage in the clubs. So was Michael Jackson. My grandmother, who is ninety-nine years old now, God bless her soul, was the life of the party. I have so many memories of her full-of-life energy. One vivid memory is of her dancing her butt off, with a straw *jíbaro* (farmer) hat that said "Puerto Rico" on the front and a can of Budweiser in one of her hands. I would stare at her admiringly and think what a cool grandmother I had. No granny knitting in a rocking chair here. Grandma Iris was a full-of-life woman who was very in touch with her sexuality and had no shame about it. I recall, at one of our house parties when I was about five years old, the music was pumping, the place was packed, and I was dancing in the crowd. Grandma Iris was drinking a beer and watching me. She called me over and in her Spanish accent said, "Andrea, *mira*, let me tell ju somsing, ju are a girl and girls have to be sexy. *Mira*, when ju dancing, yu gotta move jour hips like dis," and proceeded to show me how to shake my hips.

"Like this grandma?" I asked, doing my best to imitate her sexy womanly moves.

"Jes mama, dats it. Move those hips, *mueve la colita*." It's a great memory and to this day I can proudly say I move my hips sexy like a girl!

That was the extent of what being Puerto Rican was to me, but when I was eleven my parents sent me to Puerto Rico to spend the summer with my other grandma, Grandma Benny. I went all by myself on a plane and I got to sit by the window! It was incredible to be in the air looking down at NYC, the Empire State Building, the Statue of Liberty, and the towers of the World Trade Center. The city looked like a miniature toy set and everyone looked like ants. As we ascended, we eventually flew past a layer of white fluffy clouds and spent most of the flight above them. It was weird; it made the world feel upside down. I had never had this point of view before. As we flew, I gazed out of the window and imagined myself outside, jumping on top of those clouds, like on a trampoline, bouncing from one cloud to another or lazily lounging on top of one and ripping off a piece of fluffy cloud to eat like cotton candy. The stewardesses (that's what we called them back then) were super sweet. They would check on me from time to time to see if I wanted or needed anything. They asked if I wanted to eat breakfast and one of the options was pancakes. Woohoo, had I died and gone to heaven? Of course, I wanted breakfast and yes, "I'll have the pancakes please!" I was so excited. This trip to Puerto Rico was turning out to be great! Then—record scratch—the pancakes arrived and I disappointedly discovered what the term "airplane food" meant.

Three hours later, we approached the beautiful island of Borinquen. (I learned that Borinquen was what the original native inhabitants, the Taínos, called the island, before it was invaded by Spain. Hence why people from the island refer to themselves as Boricua.) Soaring above the lush tropical landscape, I caught my first glimpse of the calm turquoise waters of Puerto Rico. Wow! I had never seen water that color. Hugging along the coastline and cruising above the palm trees I could see why its other name was La Isla del Encanto (The Isle of Enchantment), because it was so beautiful.

Once off the plane I was escorted to the terminal to meet my grandmother. I had no idea how we were going to find her because I didn't know what she looked like. The last time I had seen her was probably when I was a baby when she was still living in NYC. Eventually we found her, along with my step-grandfather and my teenage aunt Patti. It was weird meeting them. They were complete strangers to me. Grandma Benny was blonde and had blue eyes and looked like my father. I knew my father was Puerto Rican, with white skin, light brown hair, and blue eyes, but I thought he was an anomaly—adopted or something. All the other Hispanic people I knew were dark. But there she was, this white woman who spoke Spanish and who hugged me like I was her long-lost child. As she bear-hugged me, I flinched in pain because in between us, digging into my belly, was a gift for grandma that I held in my arms. It was from my dad, an old-fashioned wooden coffee grinder, the kind that has an ornately designed cast-iron wheel that needs to be manually operated to grind the coffee. Her eyes lit up. She seemed very pleased.

We finally arrived at her house. My grandmother proudly told me that she and her husband had built the house themselves. They had immigrated to New York years back and busted their asses working, with the plan to save enough money to move back to Puerto Rico and build a home. And that's exactly what they did. It was a humble home but it was nice. The neighborhood smelled like fresh-baked bread and, in the distance, roosters crowed almost constantly. Hold up! Shut the front door! Roosters crowing? At this hour? It was the afternoon! What were they doing crowing during the day? Everyone knows that roosters crow at the crack of dawn to wake everyone up. Nature's alarm clock. That's what I learned watching *Mister Rogers' Neighborhood* on TV. TV was the original homeschooling if you were from the hood. We didn't have roosters back in The Bronx. Mister Rogers said they crow at dawn. Head scratch. It got me thinking— Mister Rogers, a white man, could be wrong?

The house was situated in a suburb of San Juan with a weird-sounding name, Bayamòn. I learned that was another Indigenous name. I had only just arrived and was already learning so much. I learned that "airplane food" means "bad food," that Puerto Rico was originally inhabited by an Indigenous people called Taínos who called the island Boriquen, that roosters crow any time of day, basically whenever they feel like it, that white people can speak Spanish, and white people don't know everything or white people can be wrong. Interesting.

That evening Grandma Benny served the most amazing meal. One I will never forget. She made *sancocho*. She said it was my father's favorite dish. *Sancocho* is a hearty stew made of tender chunks of beef, chicken, and/or pork, with root vegetables like yucca, sweet potato, plantains, and more. She served it along with white fluffy rice and slices of *aguacate* (avocado). It was the most flavorful, satisfying, and comforting meal I had ever had in my life. I felt like I had died and gone to heaven. Especially after that "airplane food" experience. I ate that *sancocho* like there was no tomorrow. I could see the pride and pleasure in my grandmother's eyes as I devoured that stew. She loved watching me eat with such gusto. She didn't take her eyes off of me. Finally, I came up for air. I was pretty full. I leaned back, put my spoon down, and opened the top button of my shorts. Well, the look that came over Grandma Benny's face. Pleasure turned to a look of dismay in two seconds flat. Grandma Benny immediately picked up that spoon and started to feed me like a baby. She said kids were starving in China, and that I had to finish everything on my plate. She kept scooping and shoveling it into my mouth until that huge bowl was empty. I could barely move. I could literally feel the food at the top of my throat. I was afraid to move for fear of it coming out. I carefully, ever so carefully, got up, sat down on the couch, opened my shorts completely, and didn't move for hours.

Grandma Benny had served me a man-size bowl of *sancocho*, probably the same amount she would've served my dad. I was very skinny, didn't weigh more than seventy pounds, and I'm sure she was determined to get some fat on my bones before she sent me back home to NYC.

Like I mentioned, the neighborhood smelled like bread because a few blocks away was a *panaderia*—a bakery. The bakery made bread all day long and the smell in the area was intoxicating. My first morning, at 7 a.m., Grandma and I went to the bakery to buy a loaf of *pan de agua* or "water bread." *Pan de agua* is a long loaf of white bread. It has a hard and crispy crust with a fluffy airy center. When we got home Grandma asked if I wanted breakfast. I enthusiastically said yes, having discovered this woman was a queen in the kitchen. Ten minutes later she called me to breakfast and placed in front of me a cup of *café con leche* (coffee with milk) and a slice of *pan de agua* with a slathering of butter in the center. I was amazed that she was serving me coffee. I thought only adults could have it. It made me feel grown up. I took a sip of the coffee and it was delicious, better than hot cocoa. I then excitedly took my first bite of *pan de agua* and nearly fell out of my chair in ecstasy. It was warm, crispy, tender, and literally melted in my mouth. I was enraptured. I basically inhaled it and immediately asked for seconds. Grandma Benny smiled, then served me another slice. I inhaled that one too and quickly asked for thirds. But this time she said no, a surprise since she seemed to derive such joy from shoveling food into my mouth. She said the rest of the bread was for

Grandpa and Patti but, if I wanted, I could have a whole loaf to myself next time if I went by myself in the mornings to pick up the bread. Bet grandma, I'm down with that!

One day grandma's brother stopped by the house in his pickup truck. He looked like the male version of Grandma Benny, but he had a somewhat weathered look. He looked strong, with broad shoulders and big calloused hands. He lived and worked on the family farm. I had no idea my family had a farm!

In the back of the truck were big burlap sacks filled to the top with beans. All kinds of beans—black, red, kidney, and coffee beans. He had come by to bring her some of the beans he had harvested. He proceeded to unload the sacks and put them on the patio. After some chitchat in Spanish he left and grandma turned to me and asked if I wanted a cup of coffee. Since arriving to Puerto Rico I had become a real coffee addict. The coffee grandma made was so so good! It was like dessert, so of course I said yes!

"Okay, *entonces ayudame*," Grandma said. "Help me carry the coffee beans to the back patio." She took an empty burlap sack, laid it out on the patio floor in the sun, and then proceeded to show me how to spread the beans out on top of it. "Okay, we need to let it bake in the sun. Go and play." About a half hour went by and Grandma yelled for me to come back. I thought she was calling me for my *café con leche*, but no. Instead she showed me how to rake the coffee beans and then sent me away again. This went on for hours. Every thirty minutes or so we raked the beans. Every so often she would bite into one of them to see if they were ready and every time she would say, "No, not ready." Finally, after what seemed like forever, she took one last bite and announced, "Ya, they are ready. *Búscame el* coffee grinder that your Papi bought for me." I ran to fetch it and she told me to sit down, hold it in my lap, place coffee beans inside the cast iron bowl, and crank the handle. Within a few minutes we had freshly ground coffee inside of the wooden drawer at the bottom of the grinder. It was so cool! She then said, "Okay, now I will make your *café con leche*," and went inside the house.

I patiently sat waiting on the patio until she finally came out with the most amazing cup of coffee. It was hot, but not too hot. It was the perfect color of light caramel with a sweet, creamy, deep, smooth, almost chocolaty taste. Again I was in taste-bud heaven. To this day I still haven't been able to duplicate that cup of coffee. It was a once-in-a-lifetime, unforgettable experience.

That month in Puerto Rico was one of the highlights of my childhood. I learned so much about my identity as a Puertoriqueña. My parents had originally offered the trip as an incentive for me to do well in school. However, my grades still sucked by the end of the school year. I thought for sure I wasn't going get to go to Puerto Rico for the summer. Thankfully my parents sent me anyway. They most likely figured it would be good for me. They were right because eleven-year-old me got to go to the island of Puerto Rico! Borinquen! La Isla del Encanto! And finally feel some sense of belonging.

> "When you embrace your difference, your DNA, your look or heritage or religion or your unusual name, that's when you start to shine."
> ~Bethenny Frankel

# Don't Judge Yourself by Your Cover

My trip to Puerto Rico at age eleven was a wonderful experience, but I still didn't have the full picture. To me being Puerto Rican was salsa music, the Spanish language, and really good food. However, as I got older, I gradually became aware it also meant that we as a people were the underdog. We were less than. I was keenly aware that brown people were many levels down in society, that we had less money, less education, less everything, and therefore less power.

When I was sixteen years old, my mother married a wonderful man, Damian, the first man I saw treat my mother with love and respect. He cherished her and still does to this day. He was from a well-to-do family of German and Irish descent. When we went to visit his family, in the house he grew up in, they were the nicest people and very welcoming, but it was like visiting a foreign land. To me, they were rich. The house was a huge white colonial, with many bedrooms, decorated nicely, and the property was vast. So much grass, and woods, with horses. Very different from the back of my building in The Bronx.

On the walls hung family pictures of Damian, his siblings, and members of his extended family. There were even family portraits that had at least a hundred people in them. I could see the pride they held for their family and family history. There were lots of old-fashioned black-and-white pictures of what looked like important white people. Most impressive was a hand-calligraphy framed family tree that seemed to extend back ages. Last, but not least, prominently and proudly hung was a picture of the Brooklyn Bridge. Apparently Damian's great-grandfather was the actual architect of the Brooklyn Bridge!

My family didn't have anything important like that.

I would hear other people boastfully say that they were able to trace their family back to the *Mayflower* or to Ellis Island.

People from Puerto Rico didn't have that. For the most part, brown and Black people don't have that unless they can be traced to kidnapped, enslaved ancestors on slave-sale registries.

When I was seventeen, I ignorantly told my dad that Puerto Rico should be happy that the US had taken over the island and "saved" it. Boy oh boy, did I step in it. Dad got angry, really angry, to the point of tears, and listed a litany of historical facts that I had never learned in school. Facts that painted the US not as the savior depicted in the news and history textbooks but as a conqueror. The fact that Puerto Rico had been under Spanish rule for four hundred years and had never experienced freedom. The fact that the US invaded and took over the island, making it a territory. The fact that the US couldn't have cared less about the people of the island or its freedom from the Spanish, but rather that the island was only valuable to the US economically and militarily because of its strategic location. My father was a proud Puerto Rican man who loved his culture. To hear his daughter say those words cut him to the quick. Full of emotion, he handed me a book, *The History of Puerto Rico,* and said: "Read it. After you read it, you come back and try to tell me that Puerto Rico should be happy the US took over. Before you make any judgments, educate yourself."

I read the book—well, not all of it, but enough to get an eye-opening understanding. Honestly, it was over my head. The writing was advanced and I wasn't used to reading text like that. However, I learned why my family looked like a United Colors of Benetton ad. We were made up of all races. I learned that the Spanish conquered the island of Puerto Rico in 1493 and that before then the dominant Indigenous culture was the Taínos, who were linked to southern Arawak native peoples of South America. I learned that in 1511 the Taínos revolted against the Spaniards, but without success, that the famous fountain-of-youth guy, Ponce de León, ordered that six thousand Taínos be shot, and survivors fled to the mountains or left the island. I learned that in 1513 the Spaniards began a massive forced transport of enslaved Africans to the island. In 1868 there was a rebellion called El Grito de Lares, demanding Puerto Rico's independence from Spain. In 1873—ten years after the Civil War which ended legal enslavement in the US—slavery was abolished in Puerto Rico. In 1898 US troops invaded Puerto Rico during the Spanish–American War and Spain gave Puerto Rico to the US under the Treaty of Paris. In exchange, the US paid Spain $20 million for Puerto Rico, Cuba, the Philippines, and Guam. It was essentially a hostile takeover. Nothing those in Puerto Rico would be happy about.

Reading that book was fascinating. My youthful ignorance forever changed. Most important, when I looked in the mirror I saw not just a brown girl from The Bronx but a girl who came from a vast history of peoples from different parts of the world. Now I understood why my mother's mother was so dark skinned and why my father's mother was so light, with blue eyes. It explained features like high cheek bones, curly/straight hair, and slamming muscular legs. I had way more in me than some *Mayflower*/Ellis Island history BS. It paled in comparison. I had African, European, and Indigenous/Asian genes. My United Colors of Benetton family finally made sense and in the most beautiful way. I had the story of the human race in my blood.

"Sometimes the poorest man leaves his children the richest inheritance."

~Ruth E. Renkel

# Claim Your Inheritance

Something happens to me when I hear conga music. I can't quite put my finger on it, but perhaps I can say it feels primal, instinctual, visceral. When I hear conga drums playing, I can't help but want to get up and move my body, move my hips, my arms, my shoulders, my head, my feet, my torso. It's like being hypnotized, the beat takes over and dictates my body's moves. It invokes a feeling of joy and invigorates me.

When the famous worldwide hit song "Conga," written by Enrique Garcia and performed by Gloria Estefan and the Miami Sound Machine, came out it perfectly captured what conga rhythms do to me.

Come on, shake your body, baby, do the conga
I know you can't control yourself any longer

Feel the rhythm of the music getting stronger
Don't you fight it 'til you tried it, do that conga beat

Everybody gather 'round now
Let your body feel the heat
Don't you worry if you can't dance
Let the music move your feet
It's the rhythm of the island
Like the sugar cane so sweet
If you want to do the conga
You've got to listen to the beat ...

A cool sidenote: What's so awesome and mind blowing is that, many years after the song was released, I actually got to meet and work with Gloria and her husband Emilio on *Jane the Virgin*. They were the nicest people and fans of our show!

My first introduction to the sounds of the conga drums was in the salsa music my family played at our house parties in The Bronx. I didn't know what I was listening to. So many instruments were playing at one time. But one hot NYC summer day, when I was about eight years old, I got to experience conga drums all on their own. My friends and I decided to walk to our local park, St. James Park, situated between Jerome Avenue and Creston Avenue in the Fordham section. St. James Park was my favorite place to go, the only place in walking distance where I could experience nature. It was a big park, with lots of benches to sit on, birds and squirrels, long, winding paths lined with tall mature trees and grass, and rich soil where I would hunt and catch earthworms.

As we entered the park, in the distance I could hear drums tapping out familiar rhythms. I picked up my pace toward the sound to see what it was. I slowed down as I got closer, the beats much louder now. I saw a group of men sitting in a circle playing conga and bongo drums. Other men and women danced to the drumbeats. They were jamming and improvising, working off of each other, having such a good time.

The sound of the drums captivated me. I had never seen or heard this before. I stood there in awe, smiling, unaware that my hips were slightly moving to the rhythm, instinctively—as Grandma Iris had taught me. The deep velvety sound of the congas as the drummers' hands hit the dried leather tops transported me. It was so familiar, and not only because I had heard it in the salsa music that played like a soundtrack in my childhood, but I believe because it invoked a memory in my cells, a genetic history that I like to think harkens me back to my African ancestors.

Those beats and rhythms survived hundreds, if not thousands, of years, through all of the tortured experiences that those ancestors endured. Drumming survived as a way of claiming agency, a big "fuck you" to the enslavers, a way of saying, "You may lock us up, beat us, hold us captive, but you will not erase all of us. Music is part of who we are and we will not let it go. We will not forget who we are." Those ancestors held onto the idea that they were still human in spite of the subhuman treatment. Do you know how strong they had to be to endure and survive as a people? Only the strongest and smartest survive.

Those genes are part of me. Those rhythms are a part of me. I am here because of them. I have inherited their strength, perseverance, and good strong genes. I am proud of that and I am absolutely grateful for the gifts they left for us, one of them being the beautiful rich rhythms of a strong noble people.

"You always had the power my dear, you just had to learn it yourself."

~Glinda the Good Witch
*The Wizard of Oz*

# Be the Captain of Your Ship

I liked high school, but I didn't have any direction and still didn't know how to be a good student. I was lost. My focus was nonexistent. I didn't even know what to focus on. I needed something to hold onto. I had an interest in the drama club, but I didn't have experience and I was intimidated by that group. They seemed so tight. I didn't know how to get in or fit in. I thought I would get rejected, so I didn't even try.

One day in PE class I finally found something to hold onto. A boy. A rebel tough guy. Marco was good looking, wore a leather motorcycle jacket, and had a disinterested "I'm too cool for school" expression. Eventually, I got him to pay attention to me and thus a two-year journey of getting lost ensued. I lost my virginity and totally lost focus on myself. High on the drug of love, all I wanted to do was spend time with Marco, who didn't value school or see a future for himself through education. School was pointless to him; he started to skip. I started to skip school too.

As I got to know Marco, I found he was moody, distant, and cold. I would try to get him to open up and connect as I saw couples do in romantic movies, but we would end up arguing. Those arguments eventually led to him hitting me. The first time, I was shocked but not surprised, as I had seen this modeled to me growing up. I didn't like getting hit, but it was familiar to me. I was afraid to leave him. What would life be without a boy? He was my anchor. My something to hold onto. I needed love and I thought a boy was the way to get that love. So, I stayed in the relationship, not going to school, just hanging out with Marco. For two whole high school years, I stayed in a relationship that was abusive and quite damaging to my psyche.

But then something happened. Marco got two pit bulls. Pit bulls were starting to become really popular in the neighborhood, as were underground dog fights. The first pit bull he got was a really cool dog he named Brooklyn. She was sweet and very loyal to Marco. I loved her. Even though she turned out to be a softy, Marco loved her too. But her sweet nature was not what he had been looking for. He wanted a tough dog that could fight and make him look good, so he decided to get another pit bull, Zara. As a puppy, Zara was tough. She immediately took alpha position in the relationship with Brooklyn, even though she was only a pup and Brooklyn was a full-grown adult dog. Zara was already trying to dominate Brooklyn. Marco was determined to rear Zara to be vicious and planned to put her in fighting matches. As Zara got older, she and Brooklyn fought all the time in the one-bedroom apartment where Marco, his brother, and mom lived. The fighting got so bad that Marco eventually had to put a gate in the apartment to separate the dogs.

One day we were hanging out in front of Marco's building when I had to go pee. I went upstairs by myself. The apartment was empty, except for Zara the mean dog. She was locked up behind the gate on the side of apartment where the only bathroom was. I went to open the gate. Then something made me hesitate. I felt a little flutter of dread in my tummy as my hand touched the lever. I thought about Zara. She had never been aggressive toward me, but I never trusted her. That was the hesitation. However, the desperate need to pee really made me push that hesitation aside. I had no choice. I opened the gate and, as I entered, I saw Zara in the adjacent bedroom. She looked at me. We made eye contact. I continued walking into the bathroom and closed the door. Two minutes later, I finished my business. I opened the bathroom door and standing right there in front of me was Zara. She had a mean look in her eyes and made a low growl. The hairs on the back of my neck stood up. I instantly knew she wanted to hurt me. She wanted to dominate me. I couldn't get past her because the gate swung in. I made a step toward her anyway. She growled again. I knew in that moment that she was going to attack me. Without thinking—and I don't know where this came from—I reached down, grabbed her by the neck and picked her up. She thrashed, her head and body writhing angrily to get loose as she tried to bite me. With all my might, holding her by the neck, I flung her through the door of the bedroom. She landed with a thud, scrambled up quickly, and ran toward me as I made a mad dash, closing the gate behind me.

Hyperventilating, my life flashed before my eyes. I stood there realizing what I had done. I had literally saved my own life. Had I not made that split-second move to get to her first, she would have attacked me, gotten me in her pit-bull jaw-locking grip, with no one in the apartment to save me. That moment woke me up. I asked myself: "Oh my god Andrea, what are you doing? Is this the life you want to lead? Is this the guy you want to be with? What do you want to do with your life?"

I was lost. I didn't know how to find my way. I didn't have self-esteem, but deep down inside I knew I wasn't living up to my potential. That was the moment I finally said, "No. I don't want this anymore. I don't want this in my life. I want better. I want a good future."

I didn't know exactly what to do or how, but from that point I started to make changes. The first change was changing my mind about what kind of future I could have. I knew in my heart of hearts that I wanted to go to college. I wanted to do something great, but I thought college wasn't for people like me from the hood, welfare recipients, or those exposed to substance abuse and violence. However, I made up my mind that I did deserve better in spite of the messages, subliminal and external, that said I wasn't worthy. I decided that it was up to me to make my life what I wanted it to be. No one was coming to save me. No knight in shining armor. I had to be my own rescuer. And that's exactly what I did, following in the shadow of my mom, who when she needed a hero became one. I broke up with Marco and never looked back. It wasn't easy to make the changes, but there was no way I was going to allow myself to go down the losing path that Marco was on. I stopped playing hooky. I did my homework, paid attention in class, and studied for tests. Simple changes. Eventually my grades improved and in a short time my name was on the honor roll. Me, the girl who was getting Z's on her report cards, was now on the honor roll. Z meant truant. I didn't even know that you could get a Z until I got that report card. Once I refocused and made school a priority, I eventually graduated. Granted, it did take me five years to do so, something I was ashamed about for a long time, but then I realized a diploma doesn't say how long it took to graduate. It just says you graduated. Period. That's all that counts, not only to the outside world but to yourself. Knowing that I completed high school and graduated, in spite of all the strikes against me, made me a winner. I realized I had to be the captain of my ship and, just like Dorothy in *The Wizard of Oz*, I had the power all along. It was up to me to take responsibility for my life. And what a beautiful life it's turned out to be.

> "Whatever you think you can do or believe you can do, begin it. Action has magic, grace, and power in it."
>
> ~Johann Wolfgang von Goethe

# You Betta Work

I wanted to attend college, but I didn't have the grade point average to get in. Not attending school for a whole year can wreak havoc on your GPA. I was paying the price as I applied to colleges and got rejection after rejection. My outlook was bleak. However, some key teachers in my high school saw my potential, in particular Mr. Wyles. He saw how I hit the reset button and went from getting Z's on my report card to getting on the honor roll. He decided to reach out to a few colleges and tell them about me and my story. One of those schools was the State University of New York College at Old Westbury.

After he'd spoken to Old Westbury about me, I was told to apply. More importantly, I was told to write an essay for the dean of Old Westbury pleading my case. Writing had never been my strong suit. It always seemed a daunting task when I had to write a composition or paper. How to go from a blank page to a string of coherent words that actually says something that makes sense? It was intimidating, but I was extremely motivated by the chance to go to college. It was my dream. So I sat down to write that essay and I poured my heart out onto the page. In my essay, I owned up to my mistakes and what I learned from them. I talked about skipping school for a whole year, being distracted by a going-nowhere boyfriend, and eventually changing my mind and actions for the better. I actually enjoyed writing it. It was emotionally cathartic for me. It felt like a prayer. I put positive, forward-moving energy onto that page and, without knowing it, out into the Universe. Then, lo and behold, the stars aligned in my favor. Based on my essay the dean wanted to meet me in person!

When we met, he told me he was impressed by my essay and asked, "Did you write it?" I was surprised and slightly offended by the question. It had never occurred to me that someone else could've written it for me. I nervously, yet proudly, said, "Yes, I wrote it." He seemed further impressed by meeting me in person, and said, "Okay, I will give you a chance and allow you to attend Old Westbury on *one condition*—that you keep your grades up. If you start failing you will unfortunately not be allowed to continue school here." Excited, I promised that I would.

I am proud to say that I more than kept my grades up. I made it to the honor roll and kept my grade point average up, graduating four years later with a Bachelor of Arts degree.

Little did I know as I poured my heart onto that page that it would ultimately lead to discovering my career path. I put pen to paper and that one simple action changed the trajectory of my life.

"And the day came when the risk to remain tight in a bud was more painful than the risk it took to blossom."

~Anaïs Nin

# Step Outside of Your Comfort Zone

Since I was a little girl, I've secretly wanted to act. Deep down inside there was a little spark of excitement when I played pretend. It's a feeling that I find difficult to explain, but we all experience it when we do what we are meant to do. It is a knowing, a gut feeling. When you think about it, it excites you. That's what the prospect of acting was for me. It was a visceral feeling, an energy inside that made me want to go forward.

However, I didn't know anyone who acted or was in entertainment. I saw few people like me on TV or in films. So I never voiced my desire to anyone; I was too scared even to admit it to myself. It wasn't a "realistic" career to choose or way to make a living. I tucked that desire away for a very long time until …

Fast forward to my first semester as a freshman in college. I had finally made it! After all I had been through, growing up in the hood, struggling with unresolved childhood trauma, leaving a toxic relationship, taking five years to graduate high school, I was finally a college student and living on campus! I was so excited for the future. I was in the driver's seat now. The world was my oyster. I didn't know what my major would be, but I wanted it to be something I was excited about. I was open to exploring what the school had to offer.

Walking down the hall one day I spotted an audition sign. They were casting for a play called *The Exception and the Rule* by Bertolt Brecht. When I saw that sign, my heart fluttered. It was almost like that moment in movies when the guy and girl make eye contact for the first time from across the room. It was a feeling that took my breath away. When my eyes landed on that audition sign, I could feel the wind blowing through my hair as I walked in slow motion, mesmerized by what I saw and heard. That sign was calling my name, "Andreaaaa, Andreaaaa, Andrea come here. There's something sparkly and shiny waiting for you." Then, like a record scratch, I immediately heard a counter voice: "You're not thinking of trying out are you? Excuse me, but bad idea. You have no acting experience. You'll fall on your face. It'll be soooo embarrassing. All the other people that will be auditioning will have experience. You can't compete against college actors." It was like a punch to the gut. The sad part was that voice was my own, inside my head.

I talked myself out of auditioning and tried to forget it. However, a week later, I still had the audition on my mind. I knew it was coming up soon. I had filed away the dates in my memory. Again, I tried to forget about it, but that feeling kept coming up, a voice that said, "Let's do that thing, that acting thing. It looks like fun." So I said to myself, "Andrea, you finally made it to college. After all you've been through, you're finally on your own. You promised yourself that you were going to try different things. If you don't try, you're going to regret it." So in spite of my fears, in spite of those negative, seemingly rational voices, I decided that I would go.

The day of the audition arrived and I was scared. I was so nervous, but I showed up anyway. I courageously went against that voice in my head. I was determined to see the audition through.

Lo and behold, the audition process turned out to be not so bad. Really nice people asked me to do some improv and read poetry out loud. To my amazement, my nerves dissipated once I was in the room. It felt so right to me to be there.

I felt good about myself after it was over. I didn't know what the result was going to be. All I knew was that I showed up. I hadn't let myself down. Whatever the outcome, I wasn't going to have regret.

One week later, the list of the "chosen ones" was posted. I ran to see if my name was up there and, miracle of miracles, there it was. *Andrea Navedo will play "The Judge."* I actually got chosen. Me. The girl with no acting experience. But I had to choose myself first.

The rehearsal process was so much fun and the performances were even more fun—right down to the first time I forgot my lines (one of many over my acting career). There we all were, on stage, in the middle of a performance. Everything was going like clockwork when all of a sudden there was silence. I thought to myself, "Oops, somebody forgot their line. Nobody's talking." After what seemed like an eternity, the silence was finally broken when another actor spoke a line that came after mine. It was then that I realized it was me! I was the one who had forgotten their line. I had gone completely blank. How embarrassing! Despite that experience, I loved being in that play. I was so happy. I had never been so excited and passionate about anything in my life before that. Performing for the first time on stage, I was in love. I said to myself, "Oh my god, I have discovered my love, my passion. This feeling is amazing!"

A week after our last performance some of the faculty of the theater department pulled me aside and asked: "So Andrea, have you picked a major yet?"

"No, no. I haven't picked a major."

"Well, would you like to be a theater major?"

"Can you do that? Is that a major?"

"Yeah, you can do that!"

"Oh my god! Yes, yes! That's what I want to do!"

Then like a recurring nightmare, that voice popped into my head again. Fear and doubt reared their ugly heads and said that I wouldn't be able to make a living as an actor, I wasn't blonde or blue-eyed, that actors don't make a living, they are notorious for being poor. But there was that gut feeling again. That knowing, deep down inside. When something resonates for you, when something feels right, it just feels right. I knew the odds were stacked against me, but I pushed that aside. I wanted to act. I needed to act, period! I was going to major in theater and I was going to take it seriously and really make a career out of it. While acting for me was so much fun, I knew this wasn't summer camp. I was in college to get an education and to make a future for myself. I was determined to pursue an acting career despite the odds.

So, I declared theater as my major. From the day when my eyes landed on that audition sign to my decision to become an actor, I began to say, "I know you exist fear, but I'm going to do it anyway. I don't want to look back with regret." Having regret that I chickened out from going to the audition would've been way worse to me than dealing with the nervous feelings of embarrassment and fear of falling on my face. I went to that audition in spite of my fears. I needed to see where going out of my comfort zone would lead. And where did it lead me? It led me toward finding my career path. It opened up a whole new world of incredible experiences with incredible people.

"Nothing will work unless you do."

~Maya Angelou

# Show Up and Own Your Shit

I was never the kid that received awards at school or the one who was picked to play on a team, but I wanted to be the person who received recognition. I felt the sting of shame and rejection many times. Not that I deserved the recognition—I wasn't doing anything to earn it. I thought I wasn't smart enough or talented enough to get awards. My cousin Katrina, who was the same age as me, was the high achiever and the winner in our family. She excelled—at ballet, at school. She even got a scholarship to attend a private high school in Brooklyn, all expenses paid! I was the under-achiever, not worthy of attention or praise. I didn't realize that was because I had to show up. I had to do the work.

I wasn't motivated. I didn't see the point. I didn't know how to study, be organized, or be disciplined. I needed guidance and accountability, but that wasn't available. Enough times of not being the "one" who gets picked or recognized and feeling like a failure led to a wakeup call, to realizing that it was up to me. No one was gonna be my savior. And even if there was a savior out there for me, I would still have to do the work. The fact of the matter was that I wasn't showing up. I wasn't studying or working hard or facing the truth. It was all up to me. *I* had to be my savior. *I* had to take action, roll up my sleeves, and get to work.

Part of being my own savior was to be brutally honest with myself and own my shit. I own up to the fact that I can be lazy. I cut corners. If there's an easy way to get anything done, that is my first choice. I own it and I can change that. I had to admit to myself my shortcomings. I had to be honest enough to know what I was really dealing with, to build up my self-awareness muscle. Then and only then could I really make positive changes. I had to face the truth that I am responsible for what I do and what I don't do. Once I figured that out my life changed for the better. It is incredibly empowering when you take a good look at yourself, when you take responsibility for yourself and your life.

There is no magic formula to success. But if there was just one piece of advice that I would give it would be to "show up." That takes effort and courage. Showing up comes in many forms.

Show up to school, show up to studying, show up to the gym, show up to the job interview, show up to writing this book. Show up even when you are so scared that you've got a trickle of pee flowing down your leg. Put your Depends on and show up! When you show up to anything that is positive and good for you, you are essentially saying that you matter, that you are important and beautiful and smart and worthy. Because you are. When you show up for *you*, amazing things happen.

Just because I'm on TV doesn't mean I've got it all together. I battle with insecurity on the daily. I certainly don't have it all figured out. My life is not "social media perfect." No one's is. My life is real, with ups and downs, but I've learned that no matter your past, no matter where you are from, you can always go inward, work on yourself and grow, even when the way forward looks scary and unclear.

Every day I make a choice to be the best person I can be. I admit that, at times, fear holds me back. Some days I don't live up to my potential. I can be lazy, procrastinate, and believe the negative self-talk. When that happens and those voices in my head say, "Andrea, you're not good enough," I get still and remember that I was born and raised in The Bronx. I remember all of the hurdles I have overcome because I showed up. That toughness, that resilience can't be denied. And then I tell myself: "I got this. I may not look pretty doing it, but I got this." And then I keep going, taking the next right step forward. Showing up.

"She remembered who she was and the game changed."

~Lalah Delia

# Be the Change You Want to See

Deciding to become a professional actor is probably one of the craziest ideas. The statistics are insane, with something like 92 percent of the profession out of work at any one time. What that figure doesn't reveal is that the same 8 percent tend to work continuously, while the 92 percent never get a look-in. I never really paid those statistics much notice. Still don't. But I wanted to give you a sense of just how crazy it could seem.

I finished my four years at the College at Old Westbury and graduated with a BA in Theater Arts with a concentration in Acting. My parents were proud of me for graduating. One thing I am grateful for is that they never said "no" when I told them that I wanted to be an actress. It's not like they were cheering me on, after all they were realistic people, but them not saying no or discouraging me from acting meant a lot to me. It was hard enough to get past my own negative thinking. I was fearful that they would be negative too, but instead they gave me advice. My mother said, "Well, okay. Just learn how to type so you can get a job that pays the bills." And my dad said, "Oh boy, I guess you'll be living with me for a while. Okay, if you're going to do this acting thing, you'll have to learn how," and he took me to a bookstore to find books about how to get a job in acting. I found *Acting as a Business* by Brian O'Neil. It was a practical actor's guide and how-to that covered everything from approaching agents to assembling résumés. I followed everything it said. It was like having a friend in the business walk me step by step. I'm forever grateful to my dad for his insight, for showing me how to educate myself to get on a path to finding my way.

I had to find a regular day job. I wanted my own apartment and to prove to myself and my dad that I wasn't going to live with him for a long time like he predicted. I was fiercely independent and liked having my own space. I also liked not having to answer to anyone. Living on campus for four years and having my own dorm room spoiled me.

I didn't have many skills to offer, but managed to find a part-time well-paying job cold calling for a financial company. Six months after I graduated, I moved out of my dad's. I managed to get my own apartment. He was surprised and I think secretly sad because he liked having me around. He said, "You always have a place to live if you ever need it," and, grateful for his offer, I said, "Thank you, Dad," and gave him a kiss goodbye, damn determined to never move back. That would've been failure for me. Happy to say that I never did.

It took me a few years to see some traction in my acting career. I had been looking through the acting trade papers and sending myself out for auditions, while at the same time looking for representation by submitting my headshot and résumé to talent agencies. Finally, two years after graduation I got signed to an agency! I was really excited. I started doing commercial print modeling which was nice bread-and-butter work. Eventually I booked a few TV commercials—Ford cars, Bounty paper towels, the NY Lottery, and more. However, I had no luck booking a television show or film, my ultimate goal.

One day, my agents called me with an audition for the long-running soap opera *One Life to Live*. Finally the opportunity I had been praying for! Acting on a popular soap was a big deal to me. I grew up watching the soaps, so the idea of being on one? I was so psyched. When I got the scenes, I immediately sat down to work on them. The character was a girl-next-door type named Linda. I was pleasantly surprised as I had not seen a Latina girl-next-door on TV before. I figured the writers and directors must have realized that that had been missing from the television landscape and were trying to make a change. I was excited because I felt like that was who I was. "This is gonna be easy for me to play," I thought to myself, "because that's me. I'm the girl next door!" I worked hard on those scenes. Over and over I drilled them until the words flowed like water. The day of the audition arrived. I picked my best "girl-next-door" outfit, got my hair and makeup on point, then I headed out the door. I hopped on the Number 1 train, got off at the 79th Street station and walked the rest of the way to ABC Studios. I stood there and looked up at the building. The big metal ABC sign was impressive, but also a little intimidating. I got slightly nervous, but I also had a confidence, an inner knowing that I was where I was supposed to be. Acting was my dream and my destiny and I was determined to be successful at it. It was just a matter of time. I made my way inside, was told to sign in, and then sent upstairs to casting.

Sitting in the waiting room along with other girls auditioning, I tried to maintain my focus. It can be nerve-racking being in a room with the "competition." I was finally called into the casting room and met the two female casting directors for *One Life to Live*. They were very nice, open, and friendly, which helped put me at ease. We chatted for a bit about where I was from, et cetera, and then they had me do my scenes. I gave it my all and had fun with it. When I finished, they sat there for a beat looking at me and then they looked at each other as if to confirm and get each other's approval. "We'd like to call you back," they said. "Can you come tomorrow?"

Eagerly, I responded, "Yes, absolutely! Should I prepare the same scenes?"

"Yes, all the same. Don't change anything."

I walked out of there so psyched. Woop woop! "I got a call back! Yes!" The next day I excitedly walked back into their office. Oddly, no one else was in the waiting room to audition. I did the same scenes for them and when I was done again they looked at each other, conferring. "Yes?" said one. And the other replied, "Yes." They turned to me and said, "So do you want this role?"

"Uh yes, yes, I want it!"

"Okay, it's yours and it starts tomorrow. Do you have time now so we can send you in for a wardrobe fitting?"

"Oh my god. Yes, I do!"

They gave me the information and I walked out of ABC Studios casting on cloud nine. My feet were barely touching the ground. I said to myself, "This is it. This is the break I've been waiting for. I am on my way!"

Exhilarated, I made it to the wardrobe fitting. I was living my dream! "Oh my god, I can't believe I just booked this job for a major television soap opera and here I am in a wardrobe fitting!" The wardrobe woman was nice, but very focused on her job—to find the right costume for Linda. As she looked at me, asking my sizes, she pulled out a mini skirt for me to put on. I was thinking, "Okay, mini skirt, interesting choice for a girl next door," but I put it on. Then she had me put on combat boots. "Weird," I was thinking, "again, unusual choice, but okay, I don't know what the story's about so …" Then she had me put on a cutoff midriff top that showed my abs and then a pair of gold bamboo hoop earrings. "Hold up, what's going on here?" I thought.

Then my inside voice became my outside voice. I said, "Umm, this doesn't make any sense. I don't understand why you're putting me in these clothes. They don't seem to fit the character that I auditioned for."

She replied, "Oh no, that's not the role you auditioned for. There isn't any dialogue written yet for your character, so they just gave you a scene from an episode that's already aired. You're playing the girlfriend of the gang leader."

My heart sank. "What?" I felt a knot in my tummy. My excitement deflated like a balloon. "The girlfriend of a gang leader?" To me the message communicated was, "You're Latina, you know, you can't be the girl next door, you're not good enough, but you can be the girlfriend of a gang leader because that's what you're worth." I left there crestfallen and confused. I didn't know what to do. I felt caught between a rock and a hard place. I had finally booked a legitimate job on television that was going to pay the rent. It was going to be a heavily recurring role that would help me qualify for health insurance. It would also give me a professional demo reel that would help me to get more work in the future. On the other hand, I would be reinforcing a negative Latino stereotype by playing the girlfriend of a gang leader. Those stereotypes have hurt my people. They have kept us down, subliminally communicating to the world and ourselves that this was all that we were worth. I felt like I had this responsibility to put positive images of my people out into the world. I was torn.

Ultimately, I decided to take the role. I did have to pay the rent and I had no health insurance. "Okay, I'm gonna take this part," I said to myself, "but I'm not gonna play the role the way it is written on the page." The script had Linda chewing gum and rolling her head, and I said to myself, "I am not going to play her like that." Throughout the months of playing Linda, I would go against what was on the page and bring my essential self to the role. I basically played me. As time went on, they started to add Linda more and more to the storylines. I was initially told the role would last about four months. It lasted for two and a half years! I truly believe it lasted that long because I did not play the stereotype that was on the page. They started to rewrite the Linda character to fit me and eventually set my character up to be a love interest for one of the main characters on the show. Had I not taken that role, I would not have had two and a half years of TV experience. That role helped build my TV acting chops and opened other doors. Ironically, years later, being the change I wanted to see ultimately led me to *Jane the Virgin*, a show that had the impact I had always wanted. With my character, Xiomara, I finally got to be part of positively changing images of Latinos in the media. *Jane* was a groundbreaking show, and not just for Latinos but for diversity across the board.

"I tried nice. And I was freaking paralyzed and nobody even noticed. So I am done with nice."

~Petra Solano
*Jane the Virgin*

# Speak Up! There's Power in Your Words

Thanks to my manager, Norman Aladjem, I was sitting in the waiting room of the CW Network waiting to have a general meeting with the heads of casting. On the walls hung TV monitors playing trailers for the current shows airing at that time. As I sat watching the trailers, I thought to myself, "Well, no surprise. A lot of white actors, but where are the brown people? I don't see a lot of brown people in these trailers. Why am I even here? They're not going to hire me, a Latina from The Bronx." But then I argued back, "Alright, Andrea, stop those self-defeating thoughts. Be quiet; don't say anything. Just be nice when you go into the meeting, in case you do have an inkling of a chance."

The ladies called me in. We sat down, shot the shit, and I felt a wonderful rapport with them. They liked me. I liked them. Then, all of a sudden, I heard myself say, "You know, I was sitting in the waiting room and I noticed that you don't have a lot of people of color on your shows." Record scratch! They were stunned, and so was I, for what seemed like eternity. In my head, I argued with myself, "Andrea, what are you doing? Shut up! You're ruining this meeting!" But then I thought, "They need to know they need some people of color in their shows." I was arguing back and forth in my head, when finally the ladies said, "We have actors of color, we have so-and-so, and so-and so, but you know what? We recognize that we need more people of color in our shows. In fact, we have a pilot coming up this pilot season called *Jane the Virgin* and you would be great for the role of the mother, Xiomara."

*Jane the Virgin* turned out to be a pivotal point in my career, but also in the Hollywood landscape. Its popularity and success helped to bring attention to the importance of diversity on TV and film. I like to think that my speaking up in that interview added to the many voices that have been bravely speaking up and demanding more diversity for decades. All the voices added up and eventually shouted down a huge chunk of the "Hollywood White Wall." Since then, we have seen a tidal wave of diversity in the media landscape. I am proud that I used the power of my words and got to be part of the change.

Many stereotypes are still in play, but I feel that we, those speaking up for change, are part of the movement that is going in the direction of more positive, or at least balanced, images.

"They need role models. Mateo is copying everything that I'm doing. Everything. And I have to look at that. What am I teaching my kids?"
~Rafael Solano<br>*Jane the Virgin*

# Represent!

Booking *Jane the Virgin* truly was a breakthrough for me. It was like giving birth. It was much pain for over twenty-seven years to get to the point in my career where I played Xiomara. I loved portraying her. She was not the stereotypical hot, sex-craved Latina I saw in TV and film growing up. She had so many colors. She was a fiercely loving and protective mother to her daughter Jane. She was also smart, funny, sexy, insecure, tough, vulnerable, and so much more. With each episode I discovered more of who she was and, in turn, more of who I was. She was a dream character and I got to play her with a dream cast and crew, uber-talented writers, and super-supportive and brave producers and network. From top to bottom we had an amazing team.

It was an honor for me to represent my Latino culture in a positive, inspiring, and authentic light on *Jane the Virgin*. Although I act for the love of it, I also know that every time I show up to an audition, job, award function, et cetera, I am representing my people and essentially saying that we matter. The younger generation especially needs to see the positive images of ourselves. I speak from personal experience. I had been emotionally and psychologically starving from the breadcrumb Latino images doled out over the years. As children we're looking for inspiration, we're looking for something to hold on to, we're looking for something to strive for, we're looking for ourselves. We want to see ourselves. If you grow up not seeing positive cultural or racial images of who you embody, the subliminal message is that you have no value, that you're not important. I felt invisible when I was growing up. I grew up in a predominantly Latino and Black neighborhood, but when I watched TV I didn't see much of us, and what I did see were negative stereotypes. When I finally booked *Jane the Virgin* it was incredible to see and *be*, as the series developed, Latino characters who were not only leading the show but were also portrayed in a beautiful, positive light. With flaws, too, yet at the same time revered. *We* were the heroes of the story. It validated the little girl in me—who's still very much there—who still wants to be valued and heard and seen and loved. I realized that *Jane the Virgin* was what I needed when I was growing up. It would have made a big difference.

But it's okay, because that wasn't supposed to be my journey. My journey was perfectly set up to make me feel the negative impact of not being valued. It forced me strive to value myself, to put myself forward, to *pick me* before society or anyone else was gonna pick me. I had to fight for *me*. Doing that empowered me to go the long haul, eventually landing me on *Jane the Virgin*, where I got to play a role that had an impact on people who were just like me, who needed to see themselves reflected in a positive light, who needed to see it to be it.

I see the value in "not having" that my Bronx girlhood created because I can now show up victoriously to tell the story and help put our people on the map. I look at my ninety-nine-year-old grandmother, my mother, and my aunts and know that some of their history and what they have had to endure is finally being shared in *Jane the Virgin* and other TV shows and films. They are finally getting to see themselves reflected in an honorable and beautiful light and I have the privilege of being able to deliver that gift to them.

I was a Latina brown girl in The Bronx, watching Brooke Shields sell jeans on my aluminum-foil-antennaed TV. Had someone whispered in my ear, "Andrea, don't worry, someday you are going to be an actress just like her. Not only that, you're going to act with her *and* she's going to be a guest on *your* show," I would never have believed it. Nevertheless, during season five of *Jane*, Brooke Shields was indeed a guest on the show. She played my nemesis. We even had a cat fight in water *à la* the prime-time TV soap opera *Dynasty*. It was freaking amazing, a full-circle moment, from that little Latina on welfare in The Bronx to being the one to represent!

# Embrace Your "Otherness"

Being of Latina heritage and being from The Bronx, which has been portrayed negatively in films, on TV, and in the news, made me keenly aware that I was the "other." It was not a good feeling. However, I now know my ancestral roots. Pride in my ancestry helps me see that where I come from is what makes me ME. I owe so much to my heritage. I see today as an opportunity to pay homage to my Puerto Rican ancestors, to represent my strong, courageous, full-of-grit Puerto Rican grandparents. I am proof that their sacrifices were worth it. They immigrated here with dreams, hoping for a better life for themselves and for their children. They endured so much. Leaving their beautiful island, having to learn a new language and culture, they were subjected to low wages, denial of rights, and racism. I come from a long line of people who have persevered.

YOU also come from a long line of people who worked hard and persevered. YOU have strong, tough, resilient genes. The genes of las Indias. The genes of las Africanas. The genes of las Españolas and more. Think of the women before us. We have those genes coursing through our veins. Strong, tough, and resilient genes.

We wouldn't be here if it wasn't for those immigrant ancestors living through slavery, living through poverty, living through denial of rights. It's up to us to recognize that and make our ancestors proud. We are living during an amazing time for women in this country. We have so much at our fingertips. Yes, we still face battles, but the biggest battle we face is the battle inside of us.

No matter where you come from, no matter your circumstances, you can achieve your dreams. Yes, the struggle is real. Trust me, I know, it is SO REAL. But you can overcome those struggles and all the odds stacked against you.

And know this—you have so much to offer. Be a positive influencer for the people in your life. Show them what courage, boldness, excellence, and bravery looks like in your "otherness." Take your otherness, your Latina-ness, your African-ness, your Bronx-ness, your immigrant-ness, whatever your otherness is, and use it to your advantage. Walk with your head high and pride in your step, knowing that no matter where you were born, where you live, or how you got there, you have strong ancestors inside of you. Embrace your "otherness." Let it arm you! It can be your secret weapon.

As the Spanish saying goes—*siempre p'alate*! Always forward!

# *Acknowledgments*

Thank you . . .

Bob Sewell, my One, for believing in me, encouraging me, and loving me like no one has ever loved me. Your support has helped me jump hurdles I never thought I could. You are a dream partner, the answer to my prayer, and the best thing that has ever happened to me.

Mom (Lucy Malone (Serrano)) for leading by example and showing me that I can do hard things.

Dad (Charlie Navedo) for teaching me to have pride in my Puerto Rican heritage, for the importance of higher learning, for exposing me to the arts, and for showing me that there was a world outside of our zip code.

Ava and Nico, for being my best teachers and helping me to be a better person. Momma loves you more than you'll ever know.

Adrienne Ingrum, my editor, for helping me to believe that I could write and for guiding and supporting me in just the right way that I needed to write this book. Forever grateful!

Andrew DeYoung and Broadleaf Books for granting me the opportunity to share my stories.

Dalia Phillips, you are a true friend in every sense of the word. So grateful to have you in my life for the past twenty-six years.

Sonya Denyse, you really are a dream developer. Thank you!

Jozanne Hutchinson for inspiring me to write through example.

Norman Aladjem. "Who the Eff* is Norman Aladjem!?! And what the Eff* does he want with me?" Norm, thank you to you and Laura for watching me on *Law & Order SVU* three nights in a row, for deciding to contact me and offer your services to be my manager. You helped change the trajectory of my life and career for the better. Forever grateful.

My other managers then and now, Ben Yazdani, Sanaz Yamin, and Ray Moheet of Mainstay Entertainment, who had and have my back in the daily grind with their uber intelligence, insight, and professionalism.

Emily Downs, my attorney, and the Meyer & Downs team.

Jennie Urman, Mark Pedowitz, and the CW Network for daring to have a Latina cast lead a show and for bringing heart, humor, and positive messaging for diversity to the Hollywood landscape.

Karyn Schorr, the bestest most badass rebel therapist in the world! (Yes, I said "bestest";)) Karyn, all of my parts love you!

James Price, John Grabrowski, and the Acting Studio for giving me a safe place to hone my craft.